YORK NOTES

D0766050

ANTONY AND CLEOPATRA

WILLIAM SHAKESPEARE

NOTES BY ROBIN SOWERBY

 Longman

 York Press

The right of Robin Sowerby to be identified as Author of this Work
has been asserted by him in accordance with the
Copyright, Designs and Patents Act 1988

YORK PRESS
322 Old Brompton Road, London SW5 9JH

PEARSON EDUCATION LIMITED
Edinburgh Gate, Harlow,
Essex CM20 2JE, United Kingdom
Associated companies, branches and representatives throughout the world

First published 1998
This new and fully revised edition first published 2004
Fourth impression 2007

ISBN: 978-0-582-82309-9

Designed by Michelle Cannatella
Typeset by Pantek Arts Ltd, Maidstone, Kent
Produced by Pearson Education Asia Limited, Hong Kong

CONTENTS

PART ONE

INTRODUCTION

HOW TO STUDY A PLAY

Studying on your own requires self-discipline and a carefully thought-out work plan in order to be effective.

- Drama is a special kind of writing (the technical term is 'genre') because it needs a performance in the theatre to arrive at a full interpretation of its meaning. Try to imagine that you are a member of the audience when reading the play. Think about how it could be presented on the stage, not just about the words on the page.

- Drama is always about conflict of some sort (which may be below the surface). Identify the conflicts in the play and you will be close to identifying the large ideas or themes which bind all the parts together.

- Make careful notes on themes, character, plot and any sub-plots of the play.

- Why do you like or dislike the characters in the play? How do your feelings towards them develop and change?

- Playwrights find non-realistic ways of allowing an audience to see into the minds and motives of their characters, for example soliloquy, aside or music. Consider how such dramatic devices are used in the play you are studying.

- Think of the playwright writing the play. Why were these particular arrangements of events, characters and speeches chosen?

- Cite exact sources for all quotations, whether from the text itself or from critical commentaries. Wherever possible find your own examples from the play to back up your opinions.

- Always express your ideas in your own words.

These York Notes offer an introduction to *Antony and Cleopatra* and cannot substitute for close reading of the text and the study of secondary sources.

CHECK THE BOOK

For a guide to the meanings of words used by Shakespeare, see C. T. Onions, *A Shakespeare Glossary* (OUP, 1911, frequently reprinted).

READING *ANTONY AND CLEOPATRA*

She shall be buried by her Antony.
No grave upon the earth shall clip in it
A pair so famous. High events as these
Strike those that make them; and their story is
No less in pity than his glory which
Brought them to be lamented. (V.2.356–61)

These words are spoken at the end of the play, which Shakespeare called *The Tragedy of Antony and Cleopatra*, by Octavius Caesar, whose victory over the forces of Antony and Cleopatra at the Battle of Actium has led to their deaths. He is conscious of his role in 'High events' and of his own 'glory' in bringing about these events. It may be that he is also saying that his glory, no less than their story, is pitiable – the utterance has an interesting ambiguity. However we take it, the two words which stand out, 'pity' and 'glory', help to define what the audience feels at the end after the grand pageant of Cleopatra's suicide. The traditional account of tragedy, derived from Aristotle's *Poetics*, singles out pity and fear as the emotions induced in the audience by the spectacle of tragedy; we feel fear as we identify with the frailty and fallibility of the tragic protagonists, and pity for the unfortunate results. Yet we also speak of 'tragic heroes' and this is certainly what we have in *Antony and Cleopatra*, a hero and a heroine of grand stature, whose deaths, whatever their frailties and fallibilities in life, might be said to celebrate a transcendent love affair that makes Caesar's success at the end seem something 'paltry' (V.2.2).

CHECK THE NET

For further information on Aristotle and tragedy and the tragic hero see http://classics.uc.edu/ johnson/tragedy/ and explore the Plato and Aristotle link; for an advanced discussion, see *Tragedy*, edited by John Drakakis and Naomi Conn Liebler (Longman, 1998).

The story of Antony and Cleopatra would doubtless have been famous without Shakespeare; it has all the ingredients of the greatest interest: love, sex, a conflict between a public role and the desire for personal pleasure, power politics, high stakes, and a clash of cultural values in the union of a mighty Roman general and a sultry oriental queen with a fatal result. But it is Shakespeare's dramatisation that has brought it vividly to life and made it for the English-speaking world almost what the story of Helen and the Trojan War was for the Greeks. 'All the world's a stage / And all the men and women merely players', Shakespeare had memorably written in *As You Like It* (II.7.139–40). Yet his Antony and Cleopatra are hardly mere players; they play out their love affair on the world stage with a magnificence not possible for ordinary mortals. After he has left Egypt, Antony sends Cleopatra a rich pearl – a 'petty present' – with the extravagant promise: 'I will piece / Her opulent throne with kingdoms' (I.5.45–6). Later, Caesar complains that this is precisely what Antony has done in making her queen 'Of lower Syria, Cyprus, Lydia' (III.6.10). Was ever woman courted thus?

One of the greatest pleasures of the play is the magnificence of its poetic language which raises the characters in the imagination and sustains their larger than life status. Most famous is the picture of Cleopatra on her barge sailing down the river Cydnus to meet Antony (II.2.196–223) which culminates in a statement of her 'infinite variety' (II.2.241).

She herself grandly envisages Antony as 'The demi-Atlas of this earth' (I.5.23), then continues her imperial vision in presenting her previous conquests of Julius Caesar and Gnaeus Pompey. Her dream of Antony after he is dead, 'His legs bestrid the ocean' (V.2.82), is similarly grand. Her response to the death of Antony, 'The crown o'th'earth doth melt' (IV.15.63), and her own words as she is about to commit suicide, 'Give me my robe; put on my crown; I have / Immortal longings in me' (V.2.279–80), sustain the regal note.

Shakespeare has endowed his strongest female character with great imaginative powers. She also prompts eloquence in others, whether they are praising or, more often, blaming her. She commands attention; characters in the play, audiences in the theatre and readers of the text cannot be indifferent to her, and it is not only male spectators and readers who have found her rare combination of contradictory qualities fascinating and alluring. Queen and gypsy, poet and fishwife, witty sensualist and artful schemer, her words and deeds can shock when she strikes and harangues the hapless messenger who comes to tell her that Antony has married Octavia; and she can move the heart and touch the spirit when she responds to the death of Antony and prepares for her own death in the final scene of the play. She is one of literature's most vibrant, arresting and paradoxical characters.

CHECK THE BOOK
The dominance of Cleopatra is reflected in a recent collection of essays in the series Theory in Practice (*Antony and Cleopatra*, edited by Nigel Wood, Open University Press, 1996), where the name *Cleopatra* on the book's cover appears in letters that are ten times the size of those in Antony's name, giving visual expression to her dominance in the text of the essays themselves.

Her 'infinite variety' is reflected in the play and it can be argued that she is the dominating character. Few other dramas are made up of such varied constituent parts. There are the contrasting worlds of Egypt as place of pleasure and the more serious world of Rome, Rome being not only the city itself but also the scenes where Roman characters and Roman business predominate.

CHECK THE BOOK

On the central contrast between Egypt and Rome, which is a major feature of the structure as the scenes shift from one location to another, see the latest Arden Shakespeare edition of the play, edited by John Wilders, pp. 28–9, where its thematic significance is discussed. It has often been remarked that Shakespeare adopts a kind of 'Asiatic' language (complex, ornate, decorative and sensuous) to express the atmosphere and values of the Egyptian world, while retaining a more austere style for the world of Rome.

Although it is conceived as a tragedy, the play is not uniformly serious and solemn. There are comic scenes in Egypt and aboard Pompey's galley when the Romans, too, show that they are capable of levity. The comic scenes have serious moments and undertones; there are hints of the ridiculous in the behaviour of the principals, or more often in the comments of their underlings, when apparently serious business is being conducted. This variety from scene to scene and the varied texture and tone within scenes may be thought to serve an artistic principle, in which variety is valued for its own sake as we might value it in a tapestry or in the composition of certain types of painting, but it may also express a philosophy of art in a deeper sense, an attitude that finds the division between comedy and tragedy to be an artificial one that impedes the fullest dramatic representation of life as we experience it.

This brings us to a general truth about Shakespeare, particularly applicable to *Antony and Cleopatra*, memorably enunciated by Samuel Johnson (1709–84). At the time, under classical influence, tragedy and comedy were kept very distinct and it was believed that Shakespeare was the supreme example of a dramatist who broke all the rules:

Shakespeare's plays are not in the rigorous and critical sense either tragedies or comedies, but compositions of a distinct kind; exhibiting the real state of sublunary nature, which partakes of good and evil, joy and sorrow, mingled with endless variety of proportion and innumerable modes of combination; and expressing the course of the world, in which the loss of one is the gain of another; in which, at the same time, the reveller is hasting to his wine, and the mourner burying his friend; in which the malignity of one is sometimes defeated by the frolic of another and many mischiefs and many benefits are done and hindered without design.

(Quoted in *Johnson on Shakespeare*, edited by Walter Raleigh, OUP, 1908, p. 15)

Such is the play's variety that it does not have a single focus, a single great event upon which it is structured, a single vision to impart or a single perspective upon the love which might be thought to be at the play's centre. This leads us to consider some of the questions that the play has prompted among critics and readers.

Although it purports to be a heroic tragedy of love, there are paradoxes at its heart which have led some to question whether it can be called such at all. In the first place, is it love? For the unsympathetic Romans, Antony's involvement with Cleopatra is a demeaning affair of the flesh, mere 'dotage'. When he has decided to leave Egypt at the beginning, Antony seems to agree: 'These strong Egyptian fetters I must break, / Or lose myself in dotage' (1.2.117–8). Does the play allow us to say with confidence that the bond between Antony and Cleopatra really transcends the unsympathetic Roman view? In this connection it is perhaps surprising to reflect that, although they dominate the action, Antony and Cleopatra are not seen on the stage much together (they are kept apart by the world's affairs; this has dramatic point, of course) and when they are together, more often than not they are quarrelling or at cross purposes, misunderstanding or deceiving each other.

The only moments of harmony between them come intermittently in the war scenes; just before it they are at one in the fatal decision to fight by sea (Act III Scene 7); after the defeat, Antony reproaches Cleopatra, but when she begs his pardon he forgives her (Act III Scene 11); when he thinks she has been flirting with Caesar's messenger, he flies into a rage, as a result of which she is forced to defend herself and he is satisfied (Act III Scene 13). The most harmonious scene between them, which may be said to be full of unspoken feeling, occurs when she is arming him for battle (Act IV Scene 4). Following victory here, he salutes her in the presence of his victorious generals (very little of their affair is presented in private). After the final defeat he blames her for betraying him (this time without foundation) in the strongest possible terms which he only retracts after he thinks she has committed suicide. As he dies, there is mutually reciprocated feeling (Act IV Scene 15), but if they are the great lovers they claim to be they could hardly be at cross purposes in the face of death. Although Cleopatra dies to meet Antony, she also dies to defeat Caesar, and it is possible, though not

CHECK THE BOOK

Many earlier criticisms stress the episodic character of the play's dramatic structure, for example A. C. Bradley in his influential study *Shakespearean Tragedy* (Macmillan, 1904), p. 70, where the play is castigated for its 'faulty construction'. The underlying assumption is often that the best construction is one that maintains the three **unities** of action, place and time, supposedly derived from Aristotle. *Antony and Cleopatra* is set in various locations and covers a time span of some ten years. The unity of the play's action is not easy to summarise: there is no single central action, like the murder of Duncan in *Macbeth*, to which all leads up and from which all the subsequent action flows. Another traditional rule broken in this play is the intermingling of comic elements within a tragic design, as remarked upon by Samuel Johnson.

CONTEXT

The historical context of the play, which was written and performed in the reign of James I, is sometimes invoked to account for its problematic dramatisation of the issues of power and authority (see H. Neville Davies, 'Jacobean *Antony and Cleopatra*' in *Antony and Cleopatra* (New Casebooks, 1994), edited by John Drakakis). Jacobean scepticism about the ordered cosmos, human motives and power relations may be thought to be equally applicable to the complex representation of love in the play, which is strongly affected by the struggle for power between the two major characters. (On this, see further **Recent readings** in **Critical history**.)

necessary, to read her manoeuvrings with Proculeius, Dolabella and Caesar as a real attempt to evade the resolution to die that she makes in the immediate aftermath of Antony's death in the final speech of Act IV.

The grandeur of the lovers' passion is predominantly an effect created by descriptions of events that are outside the play's action: when Enobarbus describes Cleopatra's first meeting with Antony (II.2.196–231); when Caesar shows disgust at Antony's enthronement of the Egyptian queen (III.6.1–11); by declarations of feeling that are made when they are apart, in particular Cleopatra's speech to her maids: 'O happy horse, to bear the weight of Antony!' (I.5.21–34); Antony's soliloquy in which he declares that he will be 'A bridegroom in my death, and run into't / As to a lover's bed' (IV.14.100–1); and Cleopatra's dream of Antony after he has died (V.2.76–92).

The same might be said of Antony's heroism. By the time of the action in the play it is a thing of the past, as Caesar recalls when he bids Antony, 'Leave thy lascivious wassails' (I.4.56). Although Antony is repeatedly called 'noble', apart from sending on his treasure to Enobarbus when he hears that he has deserted him, is there much in his actions in the play that really deserves to be called noble? What of his undertaking to Octavia, for example? In Act II Scene 3 he tells Octavia that he will behave; nearly forty lines later, after hearing what the soothsayer has to say, he has decided to leave for Egypt. There is much in his actions that is stupid, as in the case of his stubborn decision, against advice, to fight by sea, and much that is ignoble; nobody forced him to follow Cleopatra, 'like a doting mallard' (III.10.19), when she fled the scene of battle. The whipping of Caesar's messenger compounds this ignobility. After the final defeat, there is no reason for him to blame Cleopatra for a further betrayal in the savage and thoroughly ignoble terms that he does.

It can be argued, therefore, that there is a disjunction between words and deeds, that the characters do not live up to the ideal notions they have of themselves. Every reader has to decide the extent to which this is so, and, if it is so to a significant degree, whether this is indeed part of the play's design or whether it is a weakness on the dramatist's part that the play does not truly embody what purports to be its subject.

Some critics are not convinced that, although the protagonists lose the world, their noble love affair represents a transcendent value for which the world is well lost; they put stress on the political aspects of the play; after all, it does contain scenes that have nothing to do with the love affair, as when Ventidius arrives back triumphantly from victory over the Parthians and tells his fellow general that he will not seek further achievement because he is fearful of arousing Antony's envy (Act III Scene 1). It has been argued that the play has been plotted to show us what is necessary for political success. It is not, of course, that Caesar is seen as an ideal figure – almost nobody has a good word for him; it is usually said that he is cold and calculating – it is rather the case that Antony's downfall is a lesson in political failure, whatever our reading of the play. To pursue the relation between public and private as it affects the protagonists will be a profitable line of enquiry.

CHECK THE BOOK
The heroic character of the love affair is dealt with in a broad context by Reuben A. Brower in a chapter devoted to the play in *Hero and Saint: Shakespeare and the Graeco-Roman Heroic Tradition* (OUP, 1971).

CHECK THE BOOK
One of the most positive discussions arguing for the coherence of the play's design is that of Janet Adelman in *The Common Liar: An Essay on Antony and Cleopatra* (Yale University Press, 1973).

CHECK THE NET
For study of any aspect of the play and its context, the easiest starting point with comprehensive links and gateways is the web site of the Shakespeare Institute Library at **http://www.is.bham. ac.uk/shakespeare/**

PART TWO

THE TEXT

NOTE ON THE TEXT

'A booke Called. *Anthony*. and *Cleopatra*' was entered in the Stationers' Register, an official list of publications, in May 1608. It is assumed that this is Shakespeare's play. The earliest text of the play is to be found in the First Folio, an edition of thirty-six plays by Shakespeare. These were collected together by two fellow actor-sharers in the King's Men, John Heminges and Henry Condell, in 1623, some years after Shakespeare's death. Many of the other plays were also published singly in quarto editions soon after performance in Shakespeare's lifetime. There is no quarto edition of *Antony and Cleopatra*. Textual scholars report that the Folio text, from which all subsequent editions are derived, is a good one, presenting fewer problems than some other Shakespeare plays.

CHECK THE NET

A full text of the play is available at http://www.absoluteshakespeare.com

References in this book are to *Antony and Cleopatra* in The New Penguin Shakespeare, edited by Emrys Jones (Penguin, 1977, and reprinted many times). Readers who are using another edition will find that often the line numbers do not quite agree, and in some cases the discrepancies can be as many as ten or so lines. This is not because one text has more or fewer actual lines than another, but because they are counted differently. Any scene containing prose will be numbered to accord with the printing of the prose, which will vary from edition to edition, and in the case of verse different editors will count the half-lines differently. Where a speaker ends in mid-line and another speaker seems to complete the line, if the number of syllables or feet exceed that in a regular iambic pentameter, the two halves will each be given a separate line number by some editors. Spelling and punctuation will also differ in varying degrees from edition to edition depending on editorial policy concerning modernisation.

CHECK THE BOOK

For an authoritative modern discussion of the text of Shakespeare and all related matters such as the relation of the printed texts to theatrical performance, see the introduction to the Oxford edition of *The Complete Works*, edited by Stanley Wells and Gary Taylor (1988).

Different editions offer different kinds of help to the reader. Most modern editions are prepared with notes. In the case of The Arden Shakespeare, edited by John Wilders (Routledge, 1995), The New Cambridge, edited by David Bevington (CUP, 1990), and The Oxford Shakespeare, edited by Martin Neill (OUP, 1994), these are extensive and helpfully located below the text. The Arden, The New Cambridge and The Oxford Shakespeare also contain extensive accounts of the stage history of the play and of modern productions.

BACKGROUND TO THE STORY

Antony and Cleopatra is an independent play that contains within itself all that is necessary for the audience to understand it. Nevertheless characters in the play often refer back to their own past and to events in Roman history that took place before the play's action. First-time readers will more readily grasp the significance of what is happening in the play if they come to it with some knowledge of the immediate historical antecedents of the action. These antecedents had been dramatised several years previously by Shakespeare in *Julius Caesar*. Knowledge of the plot of the earlier play, which Shakespeare may have assumed in his audience, will serve as an illuminating context for what is dramatised in *Antony and Cleopatra*.

Julius Caesar opens with Caesar's return to Rome after his victory in the recent civil war with Pompey the Great (father of the Pompey who appears in *Antony and Cleopatra*). Caesar had pursued Pompey to Egypt (where he had been killed), met Cleopatra and had an affair with her resulting in a son she called Caesarion (mentioned in *Antony and Cleopatra*, III.6.6). In the opening movement of *Julius Caesar* a conspiracy is formed, headed by one of Caesar's machinating lieutenants, Caius Cassius, who recruits the idealistic Marcus Brutus to his cause by persuading him that Caesar has ambitions to deprive the Romans of their liberties. Caesar is duly stabbed to death, ostensibly in the cause of freedom, on the steps of the senate house on the Ides of March, 44BC (15 March).

The conspirators justify their actions before the people but make the mistake of allowing Mark Antony, Caesar's close friend and henchman, who had not been part of the conspiracy, also to speak. In a famous speech ('Friends, Romans, countrymen, lend me your ears', III.2.75) he turns the people against the conspirators and they are forced to flee Rome. Antony is joined in Rome by Caesar's young great-nephew and adopted son, Octavius Caesar, whom he had made his heir. They join forces to pursue the conspirators and defeat them

CONTEXT

Educated members of Shakespeare's audience were doubtless more familiar than audiences today with the facts of Roman history, which was a prominent part of the grammar school curriculum. See T. W. Baldwin, *William Shakspere's Smalle Latine and Lesse Greeke* (University of Illinois Press, 1944).

CHECK THE FILM

Roman 'nobility' is a cliché of literature and film. A notable example is the 'noble' Brutus as memorably played by James Mason in the 1953 film version of *Julius Caesar*, which also features Marlon Brando as Mark Antony and John Gielgud as Cassius.

at the Battle of Philippi in Greece in 42BC (see **Map**). The action of the play ends with Antony pronouncing Brutus's epitaph, 'This was the noblest Roman of them all' (V.5.69), in apparent recognition of the purity of Brutus's motives in the conspiracy.

Antony and Octavius, together with Marcus Aemilius Lepidus, who had been a powerful political and military ally of Julius Caesar, had split up the government of the Roman world into three: an arrangement known as the triumvirate. Lepidus was given control of Africa, Octavius was in charge of Italy and the western provinces, and Antony had control of the lucrative provinces of the east. Having conquered Gaul in the west, Julius Caesar had planned to conquer the Parthians in the east. Antony doubtless hoped to accomplish what Julius Caesar had been prevented from doing.

The action of *Antony and Cleopatra* starts when the triumvirate is under threat from internal dissension caused by friction between Caesar and Antony (as a result of Antony's distracting affair with Cleopatra) and from the external challenge posed by Sextus Pompey. It covers a nine-year period starting in 40BC, when the threatened rupture between Antony and Octavius is averted by the Treaty of Misenum. After this Antony marries his rival's sister, Octavia. The play then covers the disintegration of the triumvirate, with Lepidus losing power in 36BC, until the final defeat of Antony and Cleopatra by Octavius Caesar at the Battle of Actium in 31BC.

The play ends with the suicide of Cleopatra, whom Caesar had wished to exhibit in a Roman triumph. Subsequently Caesar returned to Rome and celebrated a triumph without Cleopatra. In 27BC he took the name Augustus and reigned as Rome's first emperor until his death in AD14. He brought peace to the Roman world, establishing what is known as the '*pax Augusta*'; this is prophesied in the play when he says: 'The time of universal peace is near' (IV.6.5).

LITERARY BACKGROUND

The breathtaking sweep of Shakespeare's imaginative treatment of the story of Antony and Cleopatra can be appreciated if his play is compared with an earlier version of the same material from Plutarch by the classically minded Samuel Daniel (1562–1619) in his closet drama *The Tragedie of Cleopatra* (1594). This was written in the form of a play but not intended for performance. Revised editions were published in 1599 and 1607. The whole play covers the events contained in Act V of Shakespeare's play. It has a moralising chorus, and Cleopatra feels guilty and complains at great length about past failings and present misfortunes. There is some psychological complexity but the action is comparatively static; even her death is narrated by a messenger.

Shakespeare may also have known the translation of Robert Garnier's tragedy *Marc Antoine* (1578). This was made by the countess of Pembroke, and her version, *Antonius*, was printed in 1592 and 1595. The constraints of the neoclassical idea of a play prevented these sixteenth-century writers dramatising the love story from a point of view that embraced both lovers in a single vision.

Shakespeare may have composed his play with a famous classical treatment of the clash between love and Roman duty in his mind. The Latin epic poem of the Roman poet Virgil, the *Aeneid*, was published after his death in 19BC, a mere twelve years after the Battle of Actium. In it, the hero Aeneas, whose mission is to lead his Trojans after the fall of Troy to a new god-given destiny in Italy, encounters Dido, queen of Carthage, when he is shipwrecked on the African coast. He falls in love with her and has to be reminded by the gods of his mission. He then does the Roman thing and leaves for Italy to found the city in Latium that is to be the parent city of Rome itself.

Virgil's first readers must have seen reflected in this myth the recent historical events involving Antony and Cleopatra, and seen in Aeneas a character who, unlike Antony, puts his public duty before his personal inclinations. The dying Antony imagines himself and Cleopatra displacing Dido and Aeneas in the underworld, presumably as the most famous lovers in the world (IV.14.53–4). This is an intriguing allusion. When Aeneas visited Dido in the underworld she refused to forgive him so that they were for ever estranged. Many from Shakespeare's more learned audience would have known this. Like the play itself, Shakespeare's relation with his sources is often problematic.

CHECK THE BOOK

Comparisons between Shakespeare and Virgil in their very different treatments of this conflict between love and duty have often been discussed. See, for example, Reuben A. Brower, *Hero and Saint: Shakespeare and the Graeco-Roman Heroic Tradition* (OUP, 1971).

**CHECK
THE BOOK**

The main source for the play is 'The Life of Antony' in the *Lives* by the ancient Greek historian Plutarch. Shakespeare dramatises known historical accounts; very little is 'invented': see *Shakespeare's Plutarch*, edited by T. J. B. Spencer (Penguin Books, 1964). This is an edition of those *Lives* of Plutarch used by Shakespeare in the Elizabethan version by Thomas North (first published with the title *The Lives of the Noble Grecians and Romans* in 1579). Shakespearean passages closely following Plutarch are printed below the translation. Most editions and critical accounts discuss Shakespeare's handling of his source. The Oxford Shakespeare prints generous excerpts from North's translation. In The New Penguin Shakespeare, extracts are usefully included where appropriate at the head of each scene or within scenes. For a brief overview of Shakespeare's reshaping of Plutarch, see the introduction by John Wilders to the latest Arden Shakespeare edition (1995).

SYNOPSIS

Act I starts in Cleopatra's palace in the Egyptian city of Alexandria. Two of Antony's soldiers, Philo and Demetrius, give a disapproving Roman perspective on what they see as the infatuation of their general with the lustful Egyptian 'gypsy'. Caesar's messenger arrives and is ignored. Antony rejects empire for love (Scene 1). As a soothsayer is telling the fortunes of her maids, Cleopatra enters, avoiding Antony, who is now listening to the messenger. Antony realises he must leave Egypt for Rome and in conversation with his lieutenant Enobarbus determines to go (Scene 2). Cleopatra then uses all her wiles to keep him, but when she fails wishes him success (Scene 3). In Rome, Caesar complains bitterly of Antony's neglect of his military and political duties (Scene 4). Cleopatra, who previously in Antony's presence has been toying or wrangling with him, in his absence reveals the true quality of her feeling for him (Scene 5).

Act II deals predominantly with the political and military threat to the triumvirate posed by Pompey. The personal rivalries and animosities of the triumvirs are reported to him (Scene 1). In the house of Lepidus there is a tense meeting between Antony and Caesar in which Lepidus tries to keep the peace. Caesar's lieutenant Agrippa proposes that a marriage between Antony and Caesar's sister, Octavia, will cement their relationship. Antony agrees. After their masters have left, Enobarbus tells Maecenas of Antony's first meeting with Cleopatra and gives his famous description of Cleopatra sailing down the river Cydnus in her barge. He says that Antony will never be able to leave her (Scene 2).

Antony is seen briefly with Octavia, offering courteous words. A soothsayer then warns him to shun the presence of Caesar, whose lustre will always outshine his. In a brief conversation with his general Ventidius, he determines to leave for Egypt, for 'I'th'East my pleasure lies' (II.3.41), giving Ventidius a commission for Parthia. Plans for the departure of the triumvirate from Rome are discussed (Scene 4). The setting changes to Alexandria, where Cleopatra, reflecting on Antony, is brought the news that he has married Octavia. In frustration and anger she beats the messenger (Scene 5). The triumvirs meet Pompey near Misenum, to 'talk before we fight' (II.6.2). They settle their differences and agree terms. Enobarbus discusses the instability of the new concord between the triumvirs with Menas, Pompey's henchman (Scene 6). The triumvirs and Pompey celebrate in a banquet aboard Pompey's galley. Lepidus is carried off drunk, Caesar retires early, while Antony is the merriest of them all (Scene 7).

Act III dramatises the break-up of the alliance between Antony and Caesar, culminating in war between them and Caesar's first victory at Actium. Ventidius enters having triumphed over the Parthians. He is reluctant to make further conquests in case he is seen to attract too much glory to himself (Scene 1). Antony and Caesar part company (Scene 2). Cleopatra questions the messenger about Octavia (Scene 3). Antony complains to Octavia of her brother's treacherous treatment of Pompey and his slighting of himself (Scene 4). Enobarbus announces that Caesar, having used Lepidus in the war against Pompey, has now deprived him of his command (Scene 5). Caesar complains to his subordinates about Antony making Cleopatra queen of lower Syria, Cyprus and Lydia. He shows a determination to stand up to Antony. He tells Octavia, who has come as peacemaker, that 'He hath given his empire / Up to a whore' (III.6.66–7) and accuses him of preparing for war. The scene now moves to Actium; Cleopatra insists on being present in Antony's camp in her capacity as the Egyptian leader. Against the advice of his generals Antony, who has the advantage on land in numbers and experience, is determined to fight by sea, where he is weakest. There is a suspicion that he is acting on the advice of Cleopatra (Scene 7). Preparations are made on both sides (Scenes 8 and 9). Enobarbus tells how Cleopatra deserted in the sea fight for no apparent reason, to be followed by Antony, who thereby brought disaster on them all. One of Antony's generals deserts him for Caesar (Scene 10).

After the battle, Antony expresses a deep sense of shame and reproaches Cleopatra for causing him to lose his honour; he nevertheless grants the forgiveness she asks for (Scene 11). Caesar rejects Antony's ambassador, saying he will only deal with the queen. He sends Thidias to try to win Cleopatra from Antony (Scene 12). When he learns of Caesar's refusal to treat with him, Antony challenges him to a duel, whereupon Enobarbus concludes

CHECK THE BOOK

The defeat of Antony and Cleopatra therefore comes at the mid point in the action of the play. Act I dramatises the main conflict in which Antony is torn between Egypt and Rome. Act II is largely concerned with politics and the shoring up of the triumvirate. Act III dramatises its break-up and the subsequent battle. The consequences are first the death of Antony, which is the climax of Act IV, and then the death of Cleopatra, with which the play ends in Act V. The divisions into acts and scenes are not in the Folio text but are introduced by subsequent editors (the first being Nicholas Rowe in 1709). For a helpful discussion see the introduction by John Wilders to the play in the latest Arden Shakespeare edition (1995).

? QUESTION

Editors make twenty-eight changes of scene in the third and fourth acts, prompting the question: how were they managed on the Jacobean stage?

that Antony has lost his judgement completely and contemplates leaving him. Thidias makes overtures to Cleopatra. Antony enters as he is kissing her hand. He falls into a rage and has Thidias whipped. When Cleopatra protests that she had no dishonourable intention, Antony determines to fight on, after 'one other gaudy night' (III.13.182). Enobarbus decides to leave him.

Act IV dramatises events surrounding the two final battles at Actium, culminating in Antony's defeat and death. Caesar scornfully rejects Antony's challenge to single combat. He orders that soldiers who had recently fought for Antony be put in his front lines (Scene 1). Antony determines to retrieve his honour in the next day's land battle and generously acknowledges the service of his followers, addressing them as if for the last time (Scene 2). The soldiers in camp hear ominous music (Scene 3). Cleopatra helps Antony to arm, and he goes off gallantly to battle (Scene 4). When news comes to him that Enobarbus has deserted, he sends his treasure after him (Scene 5). When this reaches Caesar's camp, Enobarbus feels acute guilt and decides not to fight against his former master (Scene 6). On the battlefield Antony's soldiers gain the upper hand (Scene 7). Antony jubilantly leads his troops into Alexandria, where they are greeted by Cleopatra (Scene 8). In Caesar's camp Enobarbus expires through grief (Scene 9).

On the next day preparations are made for a second sea battle (Scenes 10 and 11). After his fleet has yielded to the foe, Antony denounces the 'Triple-turned whore' who has betrayed him (IV.12.13). Cleopatra enters but retreats in the face of his rage (Scene 12). She locks herself in her monument, ordering one of her servants to tell Antony that she has killed herself, with his name the last word on her lips (Scene 13). When the still-raging Antony is told this, he decides to join her in suicide and calls upon his servant Eros to do the deed. Eros kills himself instead. Antony then falls upon his sword but fails to kill himself outright. Another servant enters telling Antony the truth about Cleopatra. He gives orders that he be taken to the monument (Scene 14). There, Antony dies in the arms of Cleopatra, who laments his death (Scene 15).

Act V begins in Caesar's camp when news of Antony's death arrives. A messenger comes from Cleopatra seeking knowledge of Caesar's intentions. Caesar, revealing that his real purpose is to exhibit her in Rome in triumph, sends Proculeius with instructions to reassure her and so prevent her from doing anything rash (Scene 1). In the monument, Cleopatra's thoughts are on suicide when Proculeius arrives with reassuring words. While they are talking, one of Caesar's men, Gallus, breaks into the monument and Proculeius disarms Cleopatra of the dagger with which she attempts to take her life. Dolabella admits that Caesar intends to exhibit Cleopatra in a Roman triumph. Caesar then enters and threatens to kill her children if she commits suicide. He demands an inventory of her treasure. This she gives him, but her treasurer, Seleucus, reveals that she has kept back a significant quantity. Caesar, in apparent friendship, permits her to keep it and reassures her of his good intentions. She determines to thwart his real plans and orders her maids to bring her regalia. A simple Egyptian countryman delivers a basket of figs in which asps are concealed. She puts on her robes and crown, applies an asp to her breast and, rejoicing that she has defeated Caesar, expires with name of Antony on her lips. Caesar enters and in his eulogy orders that the famous pair be buried together (Scene 2).

DETAILED SUMMARIES

ACT I

SCENE 1

- The play opens with Roman disapproval of Antony's infatuation.
- Antony in conversation with Cleopatra rejects empire for love.

In Cleopatra's palace in Alexandria, Philo, addressing Demetrius, his fellow Roman officer, strongly denounces Antony's love for Cleopatra. He regards it as nothing more than a demeaning infatuation with a lustful harlot which is tarnishing Antony's former greatness. Entering the room, Cleopatra demands to be told how much Antony loves her. When an attendant announces that there is news from Rome, she taunts Antony that it is a summons from his wife, Fulvia, or orders from his youthful partner, Caesar. Antony

QUESTION

A straightforward conclusion to be drawn from the synopsis concerns the extent to which Shakespeare at the end has concentrated on the fate of Cleopatra, his most powerful female character, prompting the question: where do his interests and sympathies really lie in this play?

then dismisses the claims of Rome and empire upon him, asserting that love is the nobler calling. With his thoughts on the present moment he has plans only for the evening's entertainment and is not willing to hear messengers from Rome. Demetrius is surprised that Antony can so ignore Caesar, and is sorry that his behaviour is exactly as common gossip in Rome reports it to be.

**CHECK
THE FILM**
In the 1972 BBC film of the play, directed by Trevor Nunn, as Philo speaks disapprovingly there are flashbacks to brief images of Antony and Cleopatra cavorting indecorously. This is a highly effective framing device. The film is well directed and admirably acted by the principals, but there are significant cuts which have the effect often of simplifying the play.

COMMENTARY

This scene dramatises the central situation of the play in miniature. It is structured so that the love affair is seen from a Roman perspective and framed by Roman disapproval. The romance is shown under pressure from events in the outside world, represented by the messenger from Caesar, which will eventually destroy it. The scene in part bears out the judgement of the Roman soldiers about Antony, who is manipulated by the taunts of Cleopatra into neglecting his public duty. At the same time Antony's exalted language when he talks of 'new heaven, new earth' (I.1.17) and speaks of 'The nobleness of life' (I.1.36) suggests something more than a sordid affair of lust.

A sharp **antithesis** is established between Rome as a place of soldiers and politics, where Antony has until now been a hero of great heart ('plated Mars', line 4), and Egypt as a place of pleasure (lines 46–7). Cleopatra emerges as something of a **paradox**: a 'wrangling queen / Whom everything becomes' (lines 48–9, compare with Enobarbus's account of her 'infinite variety' at II.2.241–5). In the opening sentence Philo says that Antony's infatuation 'O'erflows the measure' (line 2), exceeds what is moderate; this grand passion and its backcloth are sustained by the language and imagery (see **Language** in **Critical approaches**). 'Let Rome in Tiber melt, and the wide arch / Of the ranged empire fall!' (I.1.33–4). These lines evoke the grandeur of Rome even while they reject it.

GLOSSARY		
3	files and musters	ordered ranks
5	office	attention, duty, service
6	tawny front	brown forehead, a slighting reference to Cleopatra; wordplay on forehead and military front
8	reneges all temper	renounces all self-control

GLOSSARY	
12	**triple pillar** refers to Antony as one of the triumvirs; compare with 'wide arch' at line 33
13	**strumpet's fool** wordplay, both someone who is made a fool of by a prostitute and someone who entertains a prostitute, like a court jester
16	**bourn** boundary
21	**scarce-bearded Caesar** at this time he was twenty-three, some twenty years younger than Antony
23	**enfranchise** set free
28	**process** a summons in legal language
31	**homager** servant
34	**ranged** widespread; ordered
38	**twain** two people
39	**weet** know
45	**confound the time with conference harsh** waste time quarrelling
60	**approves the common liar** proves what the gossips say of him is true

CONTEXT

The Roman soldiers call Cleopatra a **'gypsy'** (line 10), clearly a derogatory term. In Shakespeare's day, gypsies were supposed to be of Egyptian origin; it is now thought that they originally came from India. Gypsies were associated with promiscuity and superstition.

SCENE 2

- A fortune-teller predicts the future of Cleopatra's maids.
- Antony hears of a succession of difficulties that need his attention, and he decides to leave Egypt.

A soothsayer (fortune-teller) is telling Cleopatra's maids about their future; his words are sometimes ambiguous and ominous. The women joke with him and among themselves. A first messenger announces that Antony's wife and brother have been stirring up trouble for Caesar, who has defeated them, and that Labienus, an opponent of the triumvirs, has successfully led the Parthians to the Asian coast. A second messenger announces the death of Fulvia. Antony pays her tribute and recognises that his 'idleness' (line 131) – which can also mean lasciviousness – is responsible for these disasters. He realises that he must break off from 'this enchanting queen' (line 129). He communicates his decision to Enobarbus and in a final speech also reveals the threat posed by Pompey.

CHECK THE BOOK

Bawdy humour, in particular wordplays with double meaning, is a feature of Shakespeare's language in the play, particularly in the scenes set in Egypt. Dr Johnson in his 'Preface to Shakespeare' remarked that 'A quibble was to him the fatal Cleopatra for which he lost the world, and was content to lose it.' For a fascinating explanation and analysis of Shakespeare's bawdy puns, see Eric Partridge, *Shakespeare's Bawdy: A Literary and Psychological Essay* (1955).

COMMENTARY

The mood changes abruptly from the high drama and poetry of Scene 1. In the comic opening the women speak in prose; their humour is bawdy and largely inconsequential, though it is apparent that the fortune-teller does not offer them the bright future they might wish for. Cleopatra's observation of Antony that 'He was disposed to mirth; but on the sudden / A Roman thought hath struck him' (I.2.83–4) marks a change of mood and theme. Again in Egypt there is mirth, banqueting and pleasure, while Rome represents serious business. Bad news brought by messengers (a frequent plot device) comes to Antony in quick succession; his seriousness, and therefore the gravity of the situation, is brought out in the contrast with the frivolity of Enobarbus, who speaks in prose and continues in the comic vein of the scene's opening. Antony's final speech is businesslike and shows political awareness; it has none of the extravagant language he had used when talking to Cleopatra and shows that once he has made up his mind he can be decisive and focused.

GLOSSARY	
4	**horns** the old joke about cuckolding (adultery)
20	**paint** put on make-up
25	**liver** regarded as the seat of love
33	**figs** ironic; the asps by which the women will die are brought in a basket of figs
65	**cannot go** cannot achieve orgasm
73	**loose-wived** married to an unfaithful wife
106	**mince not the general tongue** speak bluntly what everyone says
118	**dotage** infatuation; the word used by Philo in the opening line of the play
138	**let women die** let women experience orgasm, a frequent pun in this play
179	**expedience** haste; expedition
195	**serpent's poison** refers to the common belief that a horse's hair placed in water would turn into a serpent and also that a serpent did not become venomous till adult

SCENE 3

- Cleopatra uses all her wiles to persuade Antony not to leave Egypt.

Cleopatra sends Alexas to find out what Antony is doing, but not to let him know she has sent him. If Antony is serious, Alexas is to say Cleopatra is enjoying herself; if he is happy, that she is sick. Charmian advises her against crossing Antony, but Cleopatra says that is not the way to keep him. As Antony enters she feigns sickness. She persistently interrupts him. He finally tells her of the business that necessitates his going. She accuses him of play-acting. When she sees that he is remaining firm and that she has lost, she wishes him success.

COMMENTARY

Cleopatra reveals herself to be an actress of formidable range, feigning illness, turning Antony's words against him, taunting and perversely misbelieving him, while making false accusations to her own advantage. There is subtlety of interaction between the characters and their past and present when she reminds Antony of his past lyrical praise of their love: 'Eternity was in our lips and eyes, / Bliss in our brows' bent' (I.3.35–6). There is impudent irony when she says, 'play one scene / Of excellent dissembling' (I.3.78–9), for this is precisely what she is doing, and bold wit when, in response to Antony's anger, she scornfully accuses him of living up to the part of a 'Herculean Roman' (I.3.84). Shakespeare's source tells us that Antony claimed descent from Anton, a son of Hercules. Yet there is dignity at the end when she apologises and bids him triumph in victory.

GLOSSARY		
14	**breathing** utterance	
36	**our brows' bent** the arch or curve of an eyebrow	
37	**a race of heaven** of heavenly origin	
48	**scrupulous faction** distrustful party strife	
49	**condemned Pompey** he had been outlawed by the Roman senate	continued

CHECK THE FILM
In the 1972 BBC film, effective use is made of the setting in which Cleopatra moves in and out of her boudoir, which is surrounded by gauze curtains through which a perplexed Antony is intermittently separated from her, as if to suggest not only that she is in command of their relationship but also that his vision of her is clouded.

QUESTION
With this reminder is Cleopatra being sarcastic or indulging in the pathos of nostalgia?

CONTEXT
Hercules was also a well-known dramatic character on the Renaissance stage, famous for his anger and fury as well as his physical strength.

GLOSSARY

61	garboils commotions
63	vials small bottles
68–9	By the fire / That quickens by the sun that gives life
81	meetly quite good
82	target shield
85	The carriage of his chafe assumes the demeanour of an angry man
96	becomings graces; changes
97	Eye look

CONTEXT

Caesar's allusion to the 'bed of Ptolemy' (line 17) reminds Shakespeare's learned audience of the incestuous marriage arranged by Julius Caesar between Cleopatra and her young brother, who later became Ptolemy XIII. Such marriages, alien to the Jacobean world, were common in the Egyptian royal family. His reference to 'the dryness of his bones' (line 27) is an insult that would not be lost on the Jacobean audience, since it refers to what was commonly thought to be a symptom of venereal disease.

SCENE 4

- Caesar denounces Antony and makes preparations to stop Pompey.

In Rome, Caesar has received news of Antony's behaviour in Alexandria. He denounces it in conversation with Lepidus. A messenger arrives alerting them to the ever-growing power of Pompey and his followers, Menas and Menecrates, who have control of the sea. Caesar wishes that Antony might abandon his dissolute ways and return to his former greatness. He decides that it is time he and Lepidus take arms against Pompey.

COMMENTARY

The scene introduces Caesar, Antony's dominant rival. In what little he has to say, Lepidus is markedly more sympathetic to Antony than Caesar, who speaks at length about Antony's weaknesses – at such length, indeed, that he emerges as something of a puritan. Yet he makes it clear that his condemnation is made upon political rather than moral grounds: Antony is imperilling the triumvirate. His behaviour reveals him to be a man of poor political judgement. Caesar, on the other hand, thinks clearly here and acts decisively; indeed, he makes no mistakes of political judgement in the action of the play.

The scene is skilfully constructed. Once again a messenger is used to propel the action forward with news of fresh danger. The threat that requires military action prompts Caesar to recall the active soldier of old; the tribute to Antony is moving and authoritative, coming as it does from his great rival. The picture of endurance and hardship that it evokes strongly contrasts with the earlier picture of drunken dissolution. The two pictures are opposites but complement each other in their extremity, befitting the characterisation of Antony, who 'O'erflows the measure' (I.1.2). Antony is raised in the audience's estimation, while at the same time the Roman view of his character and behaviour expressed by Demetrius and Philo in the opening scene is confirmed and extended.

CONTEXT

Caesar evokes Antony's past heroism at Modena in 43BC (line 57) when, after the murder of Julius Caesar, Antony, who had been pronounced an enemy of the people by the senate, was besieged by the consuls Hirtius and Pansa (Plutarch).

GLOSSARY

3	competitor partner, but with the obvious overtones of rival
9	abstract essence
11	enow enough
20	reel stagger drunkenly along
	stand the buffet endure the blows
24	foils disgraceful actions
25	lightness levity
38	That only have feared Caesar that only remained loyal to Caesar through fear
39	discontents malcontents
44	This common body compare with Antony's contempt for 'Our slippery people' (I.2.186)
49	ear plough
52	Lack blood grow pale
56	lascivious wassails lewd drinking sessions
62	stale urine
	gilded covered with yellow scum
71	lanked grow thin
77	furnished ready

SCENE 5

- Cleopatra muses on the absent Antony, reveals her passionate love for him and receives news of him from Alexas.

Her mind wholly absorbed by thoughts of the absent Antony, Cleopatra wonders what he is doing and addresses him in her imagination. She recalls earlier love affairs with great men who adored her, Julius Caesar and Gnaeus Pompey, elder son of Pompey the Great and brother of Sextus who appears in this play. Alexas, who has been with Antony, enters bearing a pearl from 'the firm Roman to great Egypt' (line 43) with the promise that he will make her queen of many kingdoms.

COMMENTARY

After Roman politics, the change of scene to Egypt and theme to love are part of the play's variety, but the scene itself is greatly varied in texture and tone, reflecting the mood and character of its central protagonist. After Cleopatra's request for a narcotic so that she might 'sleep out this great gap of time' while Antony is away (line 5), there are comic exchanges with the eunuch, revealing Cleopatra's emotional state and her sexual longing. When Mardian assures her that he has fierce passions and can think 'What Venus did with Mars' (line 18), the mythological reference, indirectly alluding to Cleopatra and Antony, marks a change of register.

Cleopatra then delivers her first great utterance of the play as she imagines Antony on his horse. 'O happy horse, to bear the weight of Antony!' (line 21) is partly erotic in its suggestiveness, but also part of the aggrandisement of Antony. This climaxes in the allusion to 'The demi-Atlas of this earth' (line 23) and continues in the military language 'arm' and 'burgonet of men' (lines 23–4). The serpent (line 25) is an appropriate image to associate with Cleopatra, given its ambiguous associations with treachery, wisdom and mystery. The 'delicious poison' of which she speaks in line 27 follows on from the image of the serpent and expresses her consciousness of the **paradox** that she is indulging in conflicting emotions. In the rest of the speech she imperiously bids us reflect on her grand love affairs of the past.

Once again a messenger is used to provide a change of focus. Alexas's account of Antony's offer of an oriental pearl and kingdoms to go with it fully matches the grandeur of Cleopatra's imaginings. When Cleopatra asks if he is happy or sad, then concludes, 'The violence of either thee becomes' (line 60), she draws

CONTEXT

This was a favourite topic in Renaissance paintings. Botticelli (1445–1510) and Piero di Cosimo (1462–1521), for example, both show Mars, the god of war, lying next to Venus, the goddess of love, in a languid swoon. The visual implication is that Mars is pleasantly exhausted after lovemaking. As Venus is wide awake, the symbolic reading is that Mars has been subdued by a force greater than himself. Cleopatra is compared to Venus at II.2.205; Antony is associated with Mars at I.1.4.

an extravagant link between herself and her passionate lover. Her tempestuous passions are exemplified in her threat to give Charmian 'bloody teeth' (line 70) when, following her mistress's prompting, she praises Julius Caesar. Her extravagance is further revealed in her action in sending twenty messengers to Antony, and in the violent flourish with which the scene ends: 'He shall have every day a several greeting, / Or I'll unpeople Egypt' (lines 77–8). After this scene, which in its language and style recalls the opening, Antony and Cleopatra, whatever their considerable flaws, are fully established as a larger than life pair involved in a grand passion that touches the sublime.

GLOSSARY		
4	**mandragora**	mandrake, a narcotic
11	**unseminared**	gelded
22	**for wot'st thou**	for do you know
23	**demi-Atlas**	Atlas bore the earth on his shoulders; demi means half – she evidently discounts Lepidus
23–4	**arm / And burgonet**	matchless in attack and defence; a burgonet is a helmet
28	**Phoebus'**	Phoebus Apollo, the sun god
29	**wrinkled deep in time**	like Antony, Cleopatra is middle-aged
31	**morsel**	a tasty mouthful
50	**beastly dumbed**	silenced by this beast
61	**posts**	messengers
71	**paragon**	compare

ACT II

SCENE 1

- Pompey contemplates the coming confrontation with the triumvirs.

Pompey, boasting control of the sea and political popularity, is confident of success against a divided triumvirate, predicting that

CHECK THE FILM
The character of Pompey is largely omitted in the 1972 BBC film version. Does his presence contribute anything important to the play?

Antony will not stir from Egypt. News comes that Antony is in fact already in Rome. Pompey is surprised and discomfited but also flattered that his success has galvanised Antony, whom he recognises as the most effective soldier of the triumvirs. He concludes on a note of uncertainty; the triumvirs have cause enough to war among themselves, but fear may unite them against the common danger.

COMMENTARY

The scene forms a prelude to the meeting of the triumvirs that follows. It exposes political divisions and uncertainties in the Roman world. Pompey is clear-sighted about the weaknesses and rivalries within the triumvirate; he reminds us of Caesar's grievances against Antony, but also shows why Caesar needs him. His opening confidence makes the threat he poses seem urgent.

Pompey's description of Cleopatra and Egypt is similar to those given by Antony's soldiers and Caesar. The Roman view is that Antony has been bewitched (lines 20 and 22), whether literally or figuratively. Cleopatra is described as 'Salt' (line 21) – lecherous. Pompey hopes that she will 'Tie up the libertine in a field of feasts' and keep Antony's brain 'fuming' (lines 23–4). Egypt is regarded as a place of libertine (immoral) pleasures and feasting, insatiably stimulating appetite at the expense of reason and dulling not the senses but 'honour' (line 26), a value associated with Rome and military virtue. His vivid picture of the 'libertine' Antony is dramatically interrupted by the news that Antony, against expectation, still has the capacity for clear thought and swift action.

> **CONTEXT**
> Given that knowledge of the Roman history surrounding the story of Antony and Cleopatra was widespread, this example of dramatic irony (and its message about the blindness of politicians) would not have been lost on the Jacobean audience.

Once again a messenger is used to great effect, propelling the action forward with even more urgency and showing in the reaction of Pompey that Antony is still the most potent force in the Roman world. Although realistic in his assessments, it is nevertheless ironic that Pompey is shown to be wrong in all his predictions: that he will be successful, that Caesar and Lepidus are not in the field, and that Antony has become so enervated by the bewitching intoxication of sensual pleasures that he will not leave Cleopatra.

GLOSSARY

13–4	**Caesar gets money where / He loses hearts** by taxation probably, which makes him unpopular. That popularity does not guarantee success is one of political messages of the play
21	**waned lip** withered. Pompey continues with the moon metaphor that he had used when he said, 'My powers are crescent' (line 10). Actually his powers are about to wane
24	**Epicurean cooks** cooks for epicures or gourmets; Epicurus is popularly associated with the philosophy 'eat, drink and be merry for tomorrow we die'
25	**cloyless sauce** sauce so tasty that it will never satisfy. Compare with Enobarbus on Cleopatra: 'Other women cloy / The appetites they feed, but she makes hungry / Where most she satisfies' (II.2.241–3)
26	**prorogue his honour** suspend the operation of his nobler self
27	**Lethe'd dullness** the waters of Lethe in Hades (the classical underworld) induce forgetfulness
33	**amorous surfeiter** this lover given to excess
45	**'Twere pregnant they should square** it would be obvious they should quarrel among themselves

SCENE 2

- The triumvirs patch up their differences.
- The alliance between Antony and Caesar is cemented by Antony's agreement to marry Octavia.
- Enobarbus describes Antony's first meeting with Cleopatra.

In the meeting of the triumvirs, Lepidus tries to keep the peace. Caesar accuses Antony of undermining his power by causing Antony's wife Fulvia and brother Lucius to make war upon him, of slighting him by ignoring his messenger and of failing to meet his sworn obligations by refusing to send him troops when required. Antony defends himself by arguing that Fulvia, always uncontrollable, and Lucius were acting on their own initiative and not at his prompting, that the messenger had arrived at an awkward time, but that he had apologised the following day, and that his failure to send troops was more a matter of neglect. He nevertheless offers a dignified apology for these failings.

? QUESTION
The audience has no means of knowing who is in the right in this quarrel as the play gives us no objective account of the incidents under dispute. Is this a weakness in the plotting or is the truth of the matter beside the point? What is the most likely inference?

Enobarbus reminds them of their present danger, whereupon Caesar's lieutenant Agrippa proposes that they cement an accord through the marriage of Antony to Caesar's sister, Octavia. Antony readily agrees to this political arrangement. They prepare to join forces against Pompey. After they have departed, Enobarbus tells Agrippa and Maecenas about life in Egypt and describes Cleopatra's journey down the river Cydnus in her barge when she first came to meet Antony. He declares that Antony will never be able to leave her.

COMMENTARY

This scene may seem to fall into two halves without obvious connection. But this is deliberate. Nowhere in the play are the two contrasting worlds of Rome and Egypt so starkly and dramatically juxtaposed. That the brilliant description of Cleopatra should come immediately after the meeting of the triumvirs in Rome is a great stroke of art. (The description of Cleopatra is discussed in **Extended commentaries**.) If it had been delivered earlier, in Egypt, it could not have had the impact it has in this scene, where it suddenly injects the life and colour of an alternative world after the tense political manoeuvrings that have preceded it.

QUESTION
The character of Enobarbus, though mentioned in Plutarch, is largely a Shakespearean development. What function does he serve in the play?

The contrast is also linguistic and poetic. There are no flights of fancy where Caesar presides; the language of the triumvirs is graceless and formal. Coming immediately after the proposal of Antony's marriage to Octavia, who is a mere pawn in a business arrangement and is not described at all, it presents us with the spellbinding magnetism of Cleopatra to which Enobarbus and – we know – Antony are bound to return. Quite frankly, after the hard realities of Roman power struggles, who would not find relief in the seductive charms of Egypt? The exotic picture of Cleopatra that emerges is not unlike the Roman view expressed before the meeting by Pompey, except that it is presented sympathetically. That it should come from the plain-speaking and previously prose-speaking Enobarbus is also a master stroke. He had earlier refused to be diplomatic when pressed by Lepidus and had reminded Antony and Caesar that there would be time for them to quarrel after they had dealt with Pompey. His role in the play is partly that of truth-teller. His judgement at the end shows that he knows Antony as well as or perhaps better than Antony knows himself.

GLOSSARY

6	**And speak as loud as Mars** that is, speak contemptuously
9	**stomaching** resentments
25	**curstness** ill temper
38	**derogately** disparagingly. Caesar's language is harsh and formal
48	**You were the word of war** the war was about you
54	**stomach** desire
67	**snaffle** a bridle
78	**gibe** laugh, mock
115	**your considerate stone** Enobarbus will be as quiet as a stone but still have his thoughts
160	**strange courtesies** done unusual favours
170–1	**dispatch we / The business** that is, make the marriage with Octavia: note that Antony shows no reluctance
186	**a fly by an eagle** a fly compared to an eagle. There is no suggestion that Enobarbus did not enjoy himself in Egypt
192	**pursed up** put in her purse, took possession of
197	**poop** the ship's high stern
203	**beggared all description** made any description seem inadequate
211	**Nereides** daughters of Nereus the sea god, sea nymphs
216	**yarely frame the office** promptly perform the task
230	**for his ordinary** meal in an inn: the word 'ordinary' is humorously chosen
232	**great Caesar** Julius Caesar
233	**cropped** bore a child (Caesarion)
245	**riggish** wanton

CONTEXT

Marriage was frequently a means of cementing a political alliance in the Roman world. Pompey the Great, father of Pompey in this play, had made a similar political marriage in taking the daughter of Julius Caesar as his wife.

SCENE 3

- Antony promises Octavia that he will behave well in future.
- A fortune-teller warns Antony that Caesar will always be more fortunate than he will.
- Antony decides to leave Rome for Egypt.

After Antony's promise of good behaviour, made to Octavia in the presence of Caesar, Caesar and his sister depart. An Egyptian fortune-teller enters and advises Antony to go to Egypt forthwith. Antony asks him whose fortunes will rise higher, his or Caesar's. Caesar's is the unhesitating reply. The soothsayer tells him that his guiding spirit, which in itself is courageous and unmatchable, becomes fearful in the presence of Caesar, who is sure to beat him at any game of chance. Antony dismisses him and asks him to summon Ventidius, one of Antony's generals.

Alone on stage he acknowledges the truth of what he has been told. Caesar has always beaten him in games of chance. He decides to go to Egypt: 'though I make this marriage for my peace, / I'th'East my pleasure lies' (lines 40–1). He gives Ventidius his commission to act in Parthia (against Labienus: see I.2.100–4).

COMMENTARY

Much happens in this short and pivotal scene. At the beginning Antony makes a promise to Octavia, but by lines 40–1 he has decided to return to Egypt. The use of the soothsayer cleverly makes it seem that Antony is in the control of some greater force. The soothsayer, who wishes to leave Rome, may simply have told him what he wanted to hear to make him leave for Egypt, but what he says is true to Antony's experience. This is a rare soliloquy from Antony. What is foremost in his mind, and therefore perhaps his main motivation, is not love for Cleopatra but the feeling that he cannot shine in Caesar's sphere.

QUESTION
Is Antony sincere when he promises Octavia that he will behave himself?

GLOSSARY	
1	office duties
20	daemon guardian angel
33	hap chance
39	inhooped enclosed within a hoop or circle in order to make them fight

SCENE 4

- Lepidus, Maecenas and Agrippa bid farewell en route to Misenum to face Pompey.

A brief transitional scene that has the effect of keeping the main political movement of the play in the audience's mind.

SCENE 5

- Cleopatra beats the messenger who has come to tell her of Antony's marriage to Octavia.

While the triumvirs journey to Misenum, the scene shifts to Alexandria. Cleopatra is reminiscing about past pleasures with Antony when a messenger arrives from Rome. When he eventually tells her that Antony has married Octavia, she beats him and even draws a knife. He flees in terror. She regrets the loss of nobility involved in her striking an inferior. He is induced to return to confirm the news. She bids Alexas ask him to tell her about the appearance, age and character of her rival.

COMMENTARY

Much of this scene is discussed in **Extended commentaries**. The opening of the scene lightens the mood as Cleopatra recalls past frolics with Antony. The loss of control in her treatment of the messenger shows not only her tempestuous, even savage, nature, but also the true depth of her feeling for Antony.

GLOSSARY		
10	angle	fishing rod
11	betray	deceive
22	tires and mantles	headdresses and cloaks. Compare with Caesar's account of the behaviour of the lovers at I.4.4–7

continued

CONTEXT

The ambivalent feelings of Cleopatra towards Antony when she learns about his marriage are suggested by the allusion at the end of this scene to the contemporary 'trick' device of the perspective painting, which showed two quite different images depending on the viewpoint of the spectator. At lines 116–17 she identifies Antony with the god Mars and the Gorgon Medusa, a hideous monster who can turn those who look upon her to stone.

GLOSSARY

23	**his sword Philippan** the sword which Antony had used in the battle in which he defeated Brutus and Cassius at Philippi
41	**formal** ordinary, conventional
50–1	**allay / The good precedence** takes away from the previous good news
95	**cistern** pond

SCENE 6

- Pompey accepts the terms of the triumvirs.
- Enobarbus predicts the undoing of Antony's marriage and his alliance with Caesar.

CONTEXT

The political debate at the opening of the scene recalls the earlier civil war between Julius Caesar and Pompey the Great. Antony had been Julius's henchman and Octavius his heir (see **Background to the story**). The legacy of past bitterness informs the present action and gives credibility to the motivation of individuals, while putting the present conflict in the context of older historical rivalries that return to haunt the present.

Caesar asks Pompey if he accepts their terms. Pompey explains that he had opposed their power because of their support for Julius Caesar, who had fought his father, Pompey the Great, in the earlier civil war. He says that he came inclined to accept their offer of Sicily and Sardinia, on condition that he must rid the sea of pirates and send wheat to Rome, but that Antony's apparent ingratitude for favours that he (Pompey) had shown to Antony's mother had made him impatient. Antony expresses his gratitude. When Pompey says he had not expected to see him there, Antony in turn thanks him for forcing him to come and for the benefits he has thereby gained. Pompey makes the agreement and asks for it to be sealed before they 'feast each other' in turn (line 60).

Enobarbus and Menas, Pompey's lieutenant, reflect on what has happened. Menas says that Pompey has missed an opportunity and that his father would never have made such a treaty. Enobarbus agrees with Menas that Antony's marriage to the sober and dull Octavia is for the purposes of policy only and that he will go to his 'Egyptian dish' again (line 124). He predicts what in fact happens, that Antony's treatment of Octavia will be the cause of a breach between him and Caesar rather than a close alliance.

COMMENTARY

What is interesting in this scene in which the destiny of the world is settled is the interpersonal rivalry and point scoring. No great matters of policy relating to the immediate crisis that brought them into confrontation are debated. Antony's seeming ingratitude for the courtesy offered by Pompey to his mother and his occupation of the house of Pompey the Great are on Pompey's mind. Pompey cannot resist the temptation to needle Antony about Cleopatra and tactlessly mentions her previous liaison with Julius Caesar until he is stopped by Enobarbus. Caesar does not say much but is sharp and presses to a conclusion when he does speak. The conversation of the subordinates at the end confirms the sense of unease that underlies the human and political relations of their masters.

CHECK THE FILM

The 1972 BBC film condenses much of the reference to past history and omits the projected plot of Menas, thus diminishing the political dimension of the play, which as a consequence becomes more straightforwardly a **tragedy** of love. Just as Shakespeare's play mixes comedy with tragedy, so it puts the love entanglement more squarely into the realm of a political struggle than other versions of the story. There has always been a debate about the extent to which the play is as obviously political as Shakespeare's other two great Roman plays, *Julius Caesar* and *Coriolanus*.

GLOSSARY	
7	**tall youth** brave young men
10	**factors** agents
13	**ghosted** haunted. He came to Brutus on the night before the battle
18	**To drench the Capitol** with Julius Caesar's blood. The senate house where Caesar was murdered was on the Capitoline Hill in Rome.
38	**unhacked edges** undamaged swords
39	**targes** shields
58	**composition** agreement
68	**Apollodorus carried** refers to the story that Cleopatra was carried secretly to Caesar in this way
78	**plainness** directness, a characteristic of Enobarbus

SCENE 7

- On board Pompey's galley, the triumvirs and Pompey celebrate their new-found accord.

The servants mock Lepidus for his inability to hold his drink and give the impression that he is a lightweight. When the principals enter, Antony has some innocent merriment at Lepidus's expense. Menas takes Pompey aside and offers to make him 'lord of all the world' (line 61) by suggesting that he should cut the vessel's cable and kill the triumvirs. Pompey says his 'honour' (line 76) prevents him from being party to such a plot; Menas should have done the deed without telling him: 'In me 'tis villainy; / In thee't had been good service' (lines 74–5). Menas decides to leave Pompey. Antony is merry; Enobarbus orders entertainment and a drinking song. Caesar, who is not enjoying himself, has a headache and departs. Pompey declares that he is Antony's friend.

COMMENTARY

As the seriousness of the previous meeting between Pompey and the triumvirs had been punctuated by triviality, so the frivolity of this comic scene is punctuated by seriousness in the form of the projected plot of Menas. The scene casts Pompey's honour and his profession of friendship in an ironic light. He would have been quite happy to have seen Antony dead if this could have been accomplished without his complicity. In the previous scene Pompey had associated himself with the honourable Brutus and the freedom of the Republican cause for which Brutus murdered Julius Caesar. We now see that he would have been quite happy, if the conditions had been right, to have supreme power himself.

The contrast in character between Antony, who enjoys good fellowship, and Caesar, who does not, is encapsulated in the exchange in which Antony bids Caesar, 'Be a child o'th'time' and Caesar replies, 'Possess it, I'll make answer' (lines 98–9). Caesar departs with the observation: 'Our graver business / Frowns at this levity' (lines 118–9).

CHECK THE FILM

In the 1972 BBC film, the celebrations that take place in the galley scene are particularly well done. The contrast between Antony and Caesar, implicit in the text, is made very explicit in the facial contortions of Caesar and his obvious discomfiture when required by Antony to join in the dancing and merrymaking.

GLOSSARY	
2	plants fruits of their agreement; footsteps
5	alms drink the remains of drink left in the glass
6–7	pinch one another by the disposition find fault with one another as a result of their opposing characters
20	foison plenty
35	pyramises a drunken version of pyramids
57	held my cap off faithfully served

GLOSSARY	
67	**earthly Jove** sole ruler of the earth, Jove (Jupiter) rules the heavens
68	**pales** encloses
	inclips embraces
81	**palled** weakened
102	**Egyptian bacchanals** dances in honour of Bacchus, god of wine and revelry
112	**pink eyne** eyes made red with drinking
113	**fats** vats
123	**Anticked** made fools of us

ACT III

SCENE 1

- Ventidius announces his defeat of the Parthians, but declines to go further.

Ventidius, given a commission by Antony (II.3.41–3), enters in triumph having killed Pacorus, son of the Parthian king, Orodes, who had treacherously killed Marcus Crassus during negotiations in 53BC, a humiliation for Roman power. A fellow soldier, Silius, bids him make good his victory by pursuing the routed army through the Parthian empire. Ventidius remarks that Caesar and Antony have always won more through their subordinates than their own persons. He then points to the example of another of Antony's generals, Sossius, who fell out of favour after too much success in Syria, and says he would attract the envious displeasure of Antony if he achieved any greater success.

COMMENTARY

The scene shows us the political world from the view of subordinates and emphasises the degree their leaders are governed by concern for their reputations. It suggests that there are limits even to Antony's bounty.

CONTEXT

This alludes to Antony's abortive Parthian campaign largely omitted from Shakespeare's play. Antony had ambitious plans to emulate the achievement of Alexander the Great in conquering what is now Persia and the subcontinent. Featuring the realities of soldiering from the point of view of those on the front line makes an ironic contrast with the previous scene in which generals and politicians first plot and then frolic. In continuous performance as envisaged in the First Folio version, which has no act or scene divisions, the contrast is particularly marked.

1	**darting Parthia** refers to the Parthian tactic of avoiding hand-to-hand fighting by flinging spears and then shooting arrows from horseback as they retreated
22	**ambition** Ventidius is motivated by a sense of what is proper for his own advancement
27–8	**that / Without the which** in other words, discretion
31	**That magical word of war** Antony's reputation
34	**jaded** driven like worn-out horses

SCENE 2

- The triumvirs part company.

Enobarbus and Agrippa mock Lepidus. Caesar bids a sad farewell to Antony and Octavia. Enobarbus and Agrippa reflect mockingly on the emotions of their masters.

COMMENTARY

The opening sequence entertainingly suggests that there is little sincerity of feeling between Lepidus and his fellow triumvirs. Caesar is apparently sincere in his feelings for Octavia, to whom he is bidding farewell. The tearful Octavia has little to say for herself and emerges as a pawn between the two men. Indeed, Caesar refers to her somewhat egotistically as 'a great part of myself' (line 24). The remarks he addresses to Antony about Octavia serve as a clear warning. The mocking comments of Enobarbus about Antony's emotions at the end serve to suggest that all might not be what it seems in the present case.

Octavia is drawn in simple terms as the good Roman wife, dutiful and submissive to the wishes of her family, a clear foil to Cleopatra, and recognisably in line with contemporary Jacobean expectations with regard to the behaviour of women.

3	**sealing** fixing seals to the agreement
6	**green-sickness** a form of anaemia supposed to afflict lovelorn girls. Lepidus's hangover is mockingly attributed to his love for Antony and Caesar
20	**shards** dung patches between which the beetle Lepidus goes to and fro

---

GLOSSARY

26–7	**band … approof** as I would stake everything you would prove to be
28	**piece of virtue** masterpiece of virtue
35	**curious** touchy and particular
52	**were he a horse** dark horses were regarded as bad-tempered
57	**rheum** watering of the eyes; Enobarbus is being sarcastic

SCENE 3

- Cleopatra questions the messenger about Octavia.

In what is an essentially comic scene, Cleopatra asks the messenger about Octavia's appearance. Having been scared out of his wits before, he is sensible enough to give Cleopatra the answers she wants and reports that Octavia is dull and dowdy.

SCENE 4

- In Athens, Antony complains to Octavia about Caesar's behaviour and starts making preparations for war.

Relations between the triumvirs have obviously deteriorated as Antony complains to Octavia that Caesar has waged new wars against Pompey and slighted him in public. Octavia bids Antony not to believe all that he has heard or at least not to take offence. She laments that she is caught between them. He agrees to Octavia's suggestion that she act as a go-between. In the meantime he determines to make preparations for war, blaming Caesar for the rift.

CONTEXT

Shakespeare has concentrated events. In Plutarch the rift occurs over a period of time. Octavia bears children by Antony, suggesting that they have more than a token domestic relationship.

GLOSSARY

3	**semblable** similar
4	**made his will** this probably means that he was courting popular favour by making the people his heirs
6	**scantly** grudgingly
12	**Stomach** resent
24	**branchless** maimed; that is, without honour

SCENE 5

- Eros reports to Enobarbus the increasing power of Caesar.

Eros, a soldier of Antony, reports to Enobarbus the news that Caesar, having used Lepidus in the war against Pompey, has deprived him of power and imprisoned him, and that Antony is angry that one of his officers has murdered Pompey. Antony's naval forces are said to be at a state of readiness for war with Caesar.

COMMENTARY

CHECK THE FILM
The omission of scenes such as this from the 1972 BBC film deprives the play of the historical and political dimension that is crucial to Shakespeare's dramatisation of the action.

This news is important in establishing that the reason for the breakdown in relations between Antony and Caesar is not primarily Antony's desertion of Octavia, for before that occurs, Caesar has been actively establishing his power.

GLOSSARY	
7	rivalry equal power
10	upon his own appeal upon the strength of his own accusations
12	thou hast a pair of chaps a pair of jaws, which will fight like dogs for control of the world
15–16	spurns / The rush kicks aside any straw

SCENE 6

- In Rome, Caesar denounces the personal and political behaviour of Antony, who is now in Alexandria.

Caesar denounces Antony for publicly bestowing upon Cleopatra the kingdoms of lower Syria, Cyprus and Lydia (he had promised to give her kingdoms at I.5.45–7) and additionally for bestowing other kingdoms on her sons. Caesar then reports that Antony has sent accusations to Rome about him: that he had not given Antony his share of the spoils after Pompey had been deprived of Sicily, that ships Antony had lent to him had not been restored and that

Lepidus had been deposed. When Agrippa says Antony should be answered, Caesar announces that he has already done so, telling Antony that Lepidus had grown too cruel. He has offered to give up some of his gains provided that Antony gives him half of his. When Maecenas says Antony will never agree to this, Caesar curtly replies that in turn no concessions can be made to Antony over what he has gained from Pompey.

Octavia enters. Caesar remarks that she has come not attended by a great train in a manner befitting Caesar's sister but like 'A market maid to Rome' (line 51). Octavia replies that she was not constrained to do so but comes voluntarily, having heard of Caesar's preparations for war and having begged leave of Antony for the purpose. Caesar informs her of what she does not know – that Antony has returned to Cleopatra. 'He hath given his empire / Up to a whore' (lines 66–7) and has assembled neighbouring kings as allies. He bids her to be patient and let fate take its course.

COMMENTARY

Events are moving swiftly. The previous two scenes chart the causes of the war from Antony's side; this scene answers by giving Caesar's actions and perspective. Caesar emerges here as a commanding figure who plans, acts and speaks confidently and decisively. His assertion that Lepidus had grown too cruel is not supported by any of Lepidus's actions as presented or reported during the play and says more about Caesar than it does about Lepidus. The manner in which he feels Octavia, as Caesar's sister, should have come to Rome shows a proud and ceremonious concern for his own dignity. He does not mince words to spare his sister's feelings.

> **📺 CHECK THE FILM**
>
> Here the 1972 BBC film provides images of this Egyptian pageant as Caesar speaks, thus effectively providing visual evidence of the affront to Roman power, here embodied in Caesar's disapproval. The power of Caesar is also effectively magnified in the film by the portrayal of Lepidus, who emerges as a kindly if bumbling idiot who is anxious to please. The notion that he is 'grown too cruel' (line 33) carries no conviction. The disapproving reaction of Caesar to his sister's unceremonious arrival is also well managed in the film, expressing both his growing alienation and confidence.

GLOSSARY	
3	tribunal a raised platform
6	my father's son Julius Caesar had adopted Octavius, his great-nephew
20	queasy the people are sickened by
25	spoiled despoiled, plundered
	rated him allotted to him
44	an army for an usher an army to escort you; unusually extravagant language for Caesar *continued*

> **GLOSSARY**
>
> 52 **ostentation of our love** its public avowal; a pompous ostentatious notion
>
> 63 **on the wind** speedily; Caesar knows more of Antony's movements than his wife
>
> 77 **my heart parted** divided; Octavia expresses no bitterness towards Antony
>
> 95–6 **potent regiment ... us** gives his powerful authority to a prostitute who raises a tumult against us

SCENE 7

• Arguments in Antony's camp and the decision to fight by sea.

QUESTION
In Plutarch the crucial decision to fight at sea is taken by Antony 'for Cleopatra's sake'. In the play it is unmotivated. Is this change to the historical source an improvement or not?

Enobarbus tries and fails to persuade Cleopatra not to be present in Antony's camp, because he thinks she will be a distraction. Antony is surprised by Caesar's speed; Cleopatra contrasts Antony's negligence. Antony decides to fight by sea. Cleopatra supports this, but Antony's generals do not. His reason, 'For that he dares us to't' (line 29), does not suggest a considered strategy; in fact it seems rather childish, like Antony's challenge to single combat (which Canidius points out Caesar has naturally declined). Enobarbus points out that Antony is unprepared by sea and much stronger on land, but Antony is obdurate.

News comes of Caesar's further advance. A soldier urges Antony to fight on land. Again he will not listen. Canidius remarks: 'we are women's men' (line 70), implying that Antony is in the control of Cleopatra. Canidius expresses surprise at Caesar's speed and the soldier tells how his strategies have deceived Antony's spies.

COMMENTARY

Caesar's speed of action is contrasted with argument and confusion in Antony's camp. Against what sounds like good advice based on a strategic assessment of strengths and weaknesses from his generals, Antony offers no convincing reason for fighting at sea.

GLOSSARY	
3	forspoke spoken against
5	denounced against us declared against us. Caesar declared war against Cleopatra as a foreign enemy, rather than Antony as a Roman
10	puzzle confuse
13	Traduced for levity censured for frivolity
35	muleters mule drivers
36	Engrossed by swift impress hastily brought together by press gangs
38	yare ready
43	Distract divide
54	is descried has been sighted
57	power army
60	Thetis a goddess of the sea (referring to Cleopatra)
63–4	Let th'Egyptians ... go a-ducking take to the water like ducks. The Romans owed their success to the land power of their legions
76	His power went out in such distractions his army marched off in so many different divisions

CHECK THE BOOK

This scene in its slighting attitude to the feminine raises sharply issues discussed by Marilyn French in her feminist analysis of the play in *Shakespeare's Division of Experience* (Jonathan Cape, 1982).

SCENES 8 AND 9

- The two forces are lined up near Actium.

Caesar issues commands not to fight by land until the sea battle is over. Antony tells Enobarbus to set troops in sight of Caesar's battle lines.

SCENE 10

- The account of the first defeat at Actium.

A distraught Enobarbus reports the flight of Cleopatra's sixty ships. Scarus enters and tells of Antony's ignominious pursuit of her. Canidius, appalled by Antony's example, decides to take the troops under his command to Caesar's camp. Enobarbus, against his better judgement, says he will stay with Antony.

SCENE 10 continued

COMMENTARY

The defeat is put down not to the prowess of the enemy, their better tactics or simply to bad fortune but to the sheer stupidity of Cleopatra and Antony, their 'very ignorance' (line 7). When the fight was evenly balanced, or even slightly in Antony's favour, for no apparent reason Cleopatra flies 'like a cow in June' stung by a gadfly (line 14). Antony follows her 'like a doting mallard' (line 19). Cleopatra's fickleness and Antony's infatuation are the entire cause of their undoing. The contempt of their followers is expressed in their use of disease and animal imagery (pestilence, leprosy, nag, cow, mallard). Antony's behaviour is seen to be a gross betrayal of his manhood, honour and usual leadership, a terrible example that has prompted flight in others and causes Canidius to desert his cause.

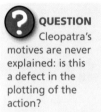

QUESTION

Cleopatra's motives are never explained: is this a defect in the plotting of the action?

GLOSSARY	
5	synod assembly
6	cantle segment
7–8	kissed away / Kingdoms the metaphor suggests the ignominious loss of empire for love
10	ribaudred wanton, lewd
14	The breese upon her a play on two meanings of breeze – wind and horsefly
17	loofed having turned her ship's head close to the wind to make herself scarce
18	The noble ruin of her magic this is the ultimate proof of the Roman view that Antony has been ruined by Cleopatra's powers of enchantment (whether figurative or literal)
23	Did violate so itself Antony's loss of honour is a violation of himself for which he bears full responsibility
26	Been what he knew himself acted like his true self

SCENE 11

- A despairing Antony is visited by a penitent Cleopatra.

Antony, shamefacedly addressing his followers, bids them take his treasure, hinting that he is bent on suicide. As Cleopatra enters, he reflects upon the contrast between what has just happened and the conduct of himself and Caesar at Philippi, where Caesar had been a mere lieutenant and he had been the chief soldier. Cleopatra begs forgiveness for her flight, offering no reason, but saying that she did not think Antony would follow. He tells her she must have known he was completely in her power but does not berate or reject her.

COMMENTARY

This is Antony's lowest point in the play. He recognises that he has betrayed and defeated himself – 'I have fled myself' (line 7) – and is in emotional, physical and moral disarray, 'for indeed I have lost command' (line 23). Nevertheless, for the first time he is honest with himself, and he shows a magnanimity in his concern for his followers and in his forgiveness of Cleopatra.

CHECK THE BOOK

In this scene in which Antony contemptuously dismisses Caesar for having worn his sword **'like a dancer'** (line 36) in the previous battle at Philippi, we see how his sense of self, his honour and his masculine identity are essentially bound up with his military prowess. He has lived by the sword and his only redemption will be to die by it. See the chapter 'Antony's Wound' in Coppélia Kahn, *Roman Shakespeare: Warriors, Wounds, and Women* (Routledge, 1997).

GLOSSARY		
3	lated	belated, like a traveller so late in his journey
13	mutiny	quarrel
15	doting	compare with 'the doting mallard' in the previous scene (line 19) and the 'dotage' of the opening line of the play
18	loathness	unwillingness
35	He at Philippi	Caesar
40	squares	troop formations, squadrons
44	He's unqualitied	he is beside himself
49	offended reputation	injured my good name
60	Thy beck	compare with Caesar's 'Cleopatra / Hath nodded him to her' (III.6.65–6)
62–3	dodge / And palter	shift and prevaricate
63	shifts of lowness	using the tricks of those who are brought low
67	My sword, made weak by my affection	the central antithesis of the play; Antony recognises the cause of his own undoing
69	rates	is worth
72	full of lead	depressed in spirit
73	viands	food

SCENE 12

- Antony seeks to make terms with Caesar, who sends Thidias to negotiate a treaty with Cleopatra.

The Jacobean audience may have been more sensitive than a modern one to the indignity implied in the status of Antony's ambassador, a mere schoolmaster. He addresses Caesar with a flowery **simile**, self-importantly drawing attention to his own unimportance. There is an obvious contrast between his treatment by Caesar and Antony's treatment of Thidias in the next scene.

Antony's ambassador requests that Antony be allowed to live in Egypt or, failing that, as a private citizen in Athens. Cleopatra asks that her heirs be allowed to inherit her crown. Caesar will not grant Antony anything. He promises to grant Cleopatra what she wishes, provided that she drives Antony out of Egypt or takes his life there. He then authorises his own ambassador, Thidias, to use virtually any means to make Cleopatra break with Antony and to observe how Antony adapts to his broken fortunes.

COMMENTARY

Caesar does not allow any sentimentality to interfere with his political interest. He shows a low opinion of women in his calculation that they are weak in misfortune.

GLOSSARY	
12	**Requires** requests
18	**The circle of the Ptolemies** the Egyptian crown
19	**hazarded to thy grace** dependent upon your favour
30–1	**want will perjure / The ne'er-touched vestal** need will make the most virtuous break her vows (the vestals were servants of the goddess Vesta and sworn to virginity)
34	**flaw** broken fortunes

SCENE 13

- Antony has Caesar's messenger whipped.
- Antony determines to fight on.

LINES 1–85

In conversation with Cleopatra, Enobarbus puts the chief blame for the present misfortune on Antony; he did not need to follow her in flight. On hearing the ambassador's reply, Antony challenges Caesar to a single fight; the ridiculousness of this causes Enobarbus to conclude that he has lost his judgement altogether. Antony departs and Thidias enters to speak to the queen. He says that Caesar knows that she embraced Antony not out of love but fear. Cleopatra agrees. Caesar, says Thidias, would like to be Cleopatra's protector. Cleopatra seems to be complying.

COMMENTARY

Much of the interest in the opening part of this scene resides in the reactions of Cleopatra. She is uncertain at the opening as she questions Enobarbus. In contrast to Antony's scorn and contempt for his rival, whom he vainly challenges to single combat – which, as Enobarbus remarks, is scarcely the action of a rational man – Cleopatra is cool and restrained, treating Caesar's messenger with courteous respect despite feeling the lack of ceremony in his approach. She speaks ingratiatingly of Caesar: 'He is a god, and knows / What is most right' (lines 60–1), falling in with the suggestion that she was constrained to yield to Antony. She is very definitely playing a political game and is ostensibly quick to yield to new realities: 'I kiss his conquering hand' (line 75).

Cleopatra may be seen to show political cunning, while the confirmation of Antony's folly is made apparent in the comment upon it by Enobarbus, who declares in an aside that Antony in imagining that Caesar would consent to single combat has lost his judgement (line 37). In a second aside he begins to question the wisdom of remaining loyal to a fool but still recognises that the person who keeps faith with a defeated master 'Does conquer him that did his master conquer / And earns a place i'th'story' (lines 45–6), that is, he conquers fortune in the noble manner of a Stoic. We are never allowed to see Cleopatra weighing moral consequences as we see Enobarbus weighing them here. Ironically, Enobarbus earns his place in the story because he chooses interest over honour and lives to regret it.

? QUESTION
What are Cleopatra's motives in her dealings with Caesar's messenger? Is she indicating to him that she will yield to his master in more ways than one? Is she flirting?

GLOSSARY		
1	Think, and die	prophetic of Enobarbus's own fate
3	will	desire, passion
5	ranges	battle lines

continued

GLOSSARY	
7	**The itch of his affection** the craving of his sexual passion
8	**nicked** maimed
10	**The merèd question** the sole ground of the dispute
17	**the boy Caesar** he is aged thirty-two at the time of Actium
22	**Something particular** some notable feat
23	**ministers** agents
26	**gay comparisons** showy advantages when compared with us (now that he has won)
37	**judgement** this opinion of Enobarbus perhaps recalls that of Caesar at I.4.33
41	**square** quarrel
71	**under his shroud** under his protection
74	**in deputation** as my proxy

LINES 85–152

As Thidias is kissing Cleopatra's hand, Antony enters (at line 85) and falls into a rage, ordering that Thidias be whipped. He berates Cleopatra. She strongly protests her continuing devotion, to Antony's ultimate satisfaction.

COMMENTARY

This reaction shows the less noble side of Antony; his treatment of Thidias recalls Cleopatra's similar treatment of the messenger in Act II Scene 5. The parallel serves to suggest a similarity in their passionate natures that are easily provoked beyond control. The beating of Thidias (and Antony's suggestion that if Caesar is offended he may beat, hang or torture his freed slave Hipparchus) is shocking and a further blot upon Antony's somewhat tarnished honour. In mitigation, it may be said that his anger has its origins in genuinely deep feeling for Cleopatra.

Her motives here and elsewhere are not entirely clear. Enobarbus is present for most of this scene and he comments on the action and judges the characters. His role here mirrors his larger role in the play up to this point.

QUESTION
Once again Cleopatra's motives are not explained. Is this a coherent dramatic strategy or a weakness in the plotting of the play?

GLOSSARY

87	**fullest** best and most fortunate
91	**muss** a scrambling game. Just as Cleopatra had complained of the lack of ceremony (line 38), so Antony is angered by his loss of authority
96	**tributaries** rulers paying tribute
105	**blasted** withered, blighted
106	**unpressed** unslept on
108	**a gem of women** Octavia
109	**feeders** servants, parasites
110	**boggler** fickle waverer
112	**seel** stitch up. Antony recognises his blindness here
116	**morsel** Cleopatra had described herself as 'A morsel for a monarch' at I.5.31
117	**trencher** wooden plate
120	**Luxuriously picked out** lustfully selected
124	**'God quit you!'** God reward you; a phrase spoken by beggars
127	**hill of Basan** the 'fat bulls of Basan' are mentioned in Psalm 22
128	**The hornèd herd** the bulls that graze on Basan or the men that Cleopatra has cuckolded
131	**yare** quick
138	**fever thee** make you shiver with fear
140	**entertainment** treatment
149	**my enfranchèd bondman** freed slave
151	**quit** get his own back
152	**stripes** marks of the whip

CHECK THE FILM
In the 1972 BBC film the contrast between the desperate jollity of the principals and Enobarbus's clear-sighted assessment of their fortunes is well brought out in the actions of Antony, extravagantly reeling with a wine cup in his hand and doting on Cleopatra, and Enobarbus, soberly addressing the camera and delivering his commentary.

LINES 153–200

After the dismissal of Thidias (line 152), Antony recovers himself. He determines to fight Caesar again by land and sea. They will drink and be merry before the fight. Enobarbus thinks Antony is attempting the impossible and that his judgement has completely deserted him. He finally decides to leave him.

COMMENTARY

As so often in this play, there is a congruity between the extremity of the language used and the extremity of the situation in which the characters find themselves. When Antony, suspecting Cleopatra of complicity with Caesar, accuses her of cold-heartedness, the extravagance of the extended hail imagery of her reply, culminating in the 'pelleted storm' (line 165), so impresses Antony that he immediately forgives her. There is indeed something paradoxical about the heat with which Cleopatra invokes coldness to deny it. Antony's own bravado in his assertion that he will kill in the forthcoming battle as many as death does in time of plague is characteristically hyperbolic, causing Enobarbus to use a corresponding hyperbole when he sarcastically remarks that Antony will 'outstare the lightning' (line 194).

GLOSSARY		
157	ties his points	laces up Caesar's clothes
161	determines	comes to an end
165	discandying	melting
167	buried them	consumed them
175	earn our chronicle	win our place in history
177	treble-sinewed, hearted, breathed	like three men in strength, courage and endurance; overblown language
178	fight maliciously	fight fiercely
182	gaudy night	festive night
190	peep through	show itself
191	There's sap in't yet	there's life in me yet
196	estridge	goshawk, a bird of prey

CONTEXT

The challenge to single combat (a Shakespearean addition to his source) is in one sense completely unhistorical, for political rivalries were no more determined by challenges like this in the Roman world than in the Jacobean. But the Jacobean audience would see it as a heroic gesture (appropriate to the epic world of Homer and Virgil) designed to show how Antony had lost his grip on reality.

ACT IV

SCENE 1

- Caesar rejects Antony's challenge.

Caesar scornfully rejects Antony's challenge. His order to put the troops who had deserted from Antony into the front lines and his description of the feast that he allows his troops as 'waste' (line 16) contrast with the generosity of Antony towards his followers and his injunction in the next scene: 'Be bounteous at our meal' (IV.2.10).

> **GLOSSARY**
>
> 8   falling the point of death

SCENE 2

- Antony addresses his followers in the knowledge that it might be for the last time.

Talking to Enobarbus, Antony determines to redeem his honour in the coming battle. He thanks his servants for their loyalty and service, bidding them treat him this night as when he was at the height of his power. He speaks of his possible death. When Enobarbus protests that he is unmanning them, he tries to change the mood, saying he was speaking for their comfort, and promises to lead them to victory.

COMMENTARY

The emotional pathos contrasts strongly with the assured calculation of the previous scene in Caesar's camp and with the violent anger which had induced Antony to beat the messenger. The scene shows Antony at his most human, introduces the theme of loyalty and lays the groundwork for Enobarbus's remorse for his desertion.

> **GLOSSARY**
>
> 8   strike surrender or hit out. Antony sees only the second meaning
> 14   odd tricks unexpected actions. Like Cleopatra, Antony is unpredictable
> 21   Scant not my cups stint not the supply of wine
> 23   suffered obeyed
> 25   period of your duty end of your obligations
> 33   yield reward
> 37   Now the witch take me let me be bewitched
> 41   burn this night with torches pass the night in revelry
> 44   death and honour the linking of these suggests that Antony feels that only in death (rather than victory) can he redeem his honour
> 45   drown consideration forget serious thoughts as we drink

QUESTION
Antony is often, as here, associated with wine, drinking and revelry. What does this reveal about his character?

SCENE 3

- Antony's soldiers hear ominous music.

CONTEXT

Musical
accompaniment
was a regular part
of the theatrical
performance of
the time. There are
also a number of
fanfares and
flourishes which
add to the dignity
of the proceedings.
See The Arden
Shakespeare,
edited by John
Wilders, p. 9.

Conversing together, a group of Antony's soldiers hear eerie music which they interpret as a sign that the god Hercules is deserting Antony. The scene forebodes inevitable doom.

SCENE 4

- Cleopatra arms Antony, who sets off for battle.

The lovers put on a brave face to one another and to the world as Cleopatra, 'The armourer of my heart' (line 7), helps Antony to arm. He is cheerful in his demeanour and actions, behaving 'like a man of steel' (line 33). Cleopatra is restrained and remarks upon his gallantry.

GLOSSARY	
2	chuck chick; a term of endearment
5	brave defy
13	daff't take it off
	hear a storm have a rough passage
14	squire a body-servant or soldier's valet. Cleopatra is more efficient (tight) than Eros
17	The royal occupation soldiering
18	workman craftsman, expert
22	riveted trim armour properly adjusted
23	port gate
32	mechanic compliment the fussy farewells of common people

SCENE 5

- Antony receives news that Enobarbus has defected, and sends his treasure after him.

Encountering the soldier who had advised him to fight by land
(at III.7.61–6), Antony admits his error. The soldier tells him of
Enobarbus's defection. Antony bids Eros send all his treasure and
after him write with friendly greetings and the hope that he finds no
greater cause to change a master.

COMMENTARY

Antony's admission of error heightens sympathy for him, as does
his response to Enobarbus's defection. His generosity is prompted
by knowledge of his own folly and by guilt: 'O, my fortunes have /
Corrupted honest men!' (lines 16–7).

SCENE 6

- In Caesar's camp, Enobarbus receives his treasure from Antony.

Caesar gives orders that Antony be taken alive and that troops
deserted from Antony should be put in the front lines. Enobarbus
reflects on the fate of Alexas (hanged) and Canidius (ill received), who
have gone over to Caesar. He already feels that he has acted wrongly
before the messenger arrives with his treasure, whereupon Antony's
bounty makes him feel acute guilt for disloyalty. He determines that
he will 'go seek / Some ditch wherein to die' (lines 37–8).

GLOSSARY		
6	three-nooked	three cornered, possibly a reference to Europe, Asia and Africa
7	olive	a symbol of peace
9	vant	van, front lines
12	Jewry	Judaea
26	safed the bringer	secured the safety of the bringer
29	Continues still a Jove	still behaves like a god (Jove was king of the gods)
33	turpitude	baseness, dishonourable behaviour
35	a swifter mean	a faster method; Enobarbus contemplates suicide if he does not die of a broken heart

CHECK THE BOOK

The recognition
of error here and
subsequently in this
final phase is a
classic feature first
prescribed for
tragedy by Aristotle.
Antony's recognition
of his error, unlike
that of other tragic
heroes, is fitful and
short-lived. He has
few self-reflecting
soliloquies and it can
be argued that he
dies with his illusions
intact. For a brief
résumé of the many
discussions, see
'The question of the
tragic' in the latest
Arden Shakespeare
edition, edited by
John Wilders,
pp. 43–9.

SCENE 7

- Antony is victorious.

Caesar retires in trouble. Against expectation, Antony and Scarus enter wounded but jubilantly, and in soldierly fashion, boasting of victory.

GLOSSARY		
6	clouts	cloths, bandages
9	bench-holes	holes of a latrine
10	scotches	gashes
12	score	cut notches in

SCENE 8

CONTEXT

This scene invites vivid musical accompaniment of drum and trumpet.

- Antony enters Alexandria and triumphantly greets Cleopatra.

Antony thanks his troops, greets Cleopatra and bids her kiss the hand of Scarus, to whom he pays generous tribute for his part in their victory. She replies that she will give him a suit of gold armour. Antony, in a vibrant speech full of the sound of celebration, bids Cleopatra join him in a triumphant progress through the streets of Alexandria to the sound of trumpets.

GLOSSARY	
2	gests achievements
7	Hectors Hector was the eldest son of King Priam, Troy's chief fighter, on whom the city depended
8	clip embrace
10	congealment congealed blood. There are many references to the actualities of wounds and fighting in these scenes
12	great fairy enchantress; a word with archaic and romantic associations
14	Chain mine armed neck put your arms round my neck in a hug

GLOSSARY

15	**proof of harness** impenetrable armour
19–20	**grey ... brown** compare with the reference to his hair at III.11.13
22	**Behold this man** Scarus
28	**carbuncled** jewelled
29	**Phoebus' car** the chariot of Phoebus Apollo, the sun god
31	**hacked targets** battered shields
33	**To camp** to accommodate; Antony's response here may be contrasted with Caesar's feeling that the feast which his men deserve is nevertheless a 'waste' (IV.1.16)
35	**royal peril** supreme danger

SCENE 9

- The death of Enobarbus.

After the fanfare upon which the last scene ends, the setting shifts in dramatic contrast to the hushed quiet of Caesar's camp on the same night. Two watchmen are reflecting on the day's defeat when they come upon Enobarbus in a state of acute depression. He poignantly addresses the moon, the 'sovereign mistress of true melancholy' (line 12), as it is associated with mental instability and madness, and asks her to witness his repentance and asks for Antony's forgiveness. He does not seek to excuse his fault. He then dies. The watchmen take his body to the camp.

GLOSSARY

5	**shrewd** harmful
8–9	**When men revolted ... memory** when deserters shall be remembered with hatred
13	**poisonous damp of night** dampness that induces sickness; part of his death wish
	disponge drop
17	**being dried with grief** the Elizabethans believed that grief dried the heart

CONTEXT

There is an abrupt change of mood as the scene shifts from celebration at Alexandria to the gloom of Caesar's camp and the depressed Enobarbus. This juxtaposition of contrasting moods and scenes (particularly prominent in Acts III and IV as the action shifts from one side to another) is facilitated by the conditions of performance on an open stage without scenery.

SCENES 10 AND 11

- Preparations for a second sea battle.

These two short scenes give notice that the coming battle is to be by sea; these are Caesar's tactics. Antony is confident to meet Caesar in any element. Caesar gives orders that a land fight is to be avoided unless Antony attacks. The implication is again that Antony's tactics do not match his other soldierly virtues.

SCENE 12

- Cleopatra's fleet deserts, resulting in a second and final rout by sea.

QUESTION
This second desertion, recalling that in the first battle (Act III Scene 10) is also not explained. Is this a strength or a weakness in the plotting?

Antony goes off to find out if the sea battle has commenced. Scarus then tells of strange omens connected with Cleopatra's fleet. Antony enters announcing that all is lost; he has been betrayed by Cleopatra (it is not clear that this is in fact so) and his fleet has surrendered. He vows revenge upon her and in his anger denounces her in strong terms. She enters but dare not approach him.

COMMENTARY

In the extremity of his anger Antony adopts the unsympathetic Roman view of Cleopatra, calling her a whore and a gypsy (compare with Philo at I.1.10). In also calling her a 'charm' (line 16) and saying that she is a 'grave charm, / Whose eye becked forth my wars' (lines 25–6), he uses language that suggests the darker side of her enchantment. He later calls her a witch (line 47), recalling Caesar's comment: 'Cleopatra / Hath nodded him to her' (III.6.65–6).

The identification of Antony with the mythical Hercules is well made when Antony says that 'The shirt of Nessus is upon me' (line 43). He sees himself being destroyed by Cleopatra as Hercules was destroyed by his lover Deianeira. There is an ironic contrast between those scenes in which Antony is loyal to his followers and inspires their loyalty and this sudden change of fortune in which he sees his followers fawning to Caesar.

CONTEXT

'The shirt of Nessus' is one of the many apposite allusions to classical mythology in the play. The centaur Nessus gave a shirt impregnated with poison to Deianeira, telling her it was a love potion that would win back Hercules's love. In fact it consumed him alive. Lichas, the messenger who brought the shirt to Hercules, was hurled by him in his death agony into the sea. Such allusions would have been more familiar to learned members of Shakespeare's audience through their education, which was much more classically based than now.

GLOSSARY	
4	**augurers** those who interpret omens, usually by the flight and behaviour of birds
8	**fretted** chequered
13	**Triple-turned whore!** perhaps because she had moved from Julius Caesar to Gnaeus Pompey and to Antony
14	**novice** inexperienced youth
21	**spanieled** fawned
22	**discandy** become liquid
23	**this pine is barked** this pine tree (Antony himself) is stripped bare
27	**Whose bosom was my crownet, my chief end** whose love was the crown and chief object of all I did
33	**blemish Caesar's triumph** spoil Caesar's triumph by killing Cleopatra so that Caesar could not exhibit her in his official triumphal procession on his return to Rome (see V.1.65–6 and V.2.109–10)
34	**plebeians** the common people
35	**spot** blemish
37	**For poor'st diminutives** for the most insignificant people (whom Antony imagines would most enjoy this spectacle)
38	**Patient Octavia** this is very much the conception on which her character is based
46	**the heaviest club** refers to the club that was Hercules's attribute. Antony is contemplating suicide, an honourable death in the Roman tradition, as well as death for Cleopatra
48	**the young Roman boy** Antony repeatedly stresses the youth of his opponent

SCENE 13

- Cleopatra retreats to the monument.

Afraid of Antony's wrath, Cleopatra seeks shelter in the funeral monument she had built for herself. She sends Mardian to tell

Antony that she has committed suicide with his name the last word on her dying lips, and to observe how he takes the news.

GLOSSARY	
2	**Telamon** when he had been defeated by Ulysses in a contest for the arms of the dead Achilles, among which was the famous shield, Ajax, the son of Telamon, went mad and killed himself
	the boar of Thessaly sent by Artemis to ravage Calydon when King Oeneus omitted sacrifices to her
3	**embossed** foaming at the mouth
5	**rive** rend, cleave
6	**going off** departing

SCENE 14

- Antony attempts suicide.

CONTEXT

Although suicide has always been considered a sin in the Christian world, for the Romans it was an honourable course; in the Stoic tradition it was considered a way of exerting control over misfortune.

Antony is conversing with Eros when Mardian enters to give the message that Cleopatra has committed suicide with Antony's name on her dying lips. Antony orders Mardian to depart and Eros to take off his armour. He asks Eros to leave him for a while. Alone on stage he begs Cleopatra's pardon and vows to join her. He summons Eros and tells him that his life after the death of Cleopatra is dishonourable and requires Eros to execute his promise to kill him. Eros refuses. Antony holds out the alternative prospect for them both of being exhibited in Caesar's triumph in Rome.

Eros asks Antony to turn away, bids him farewell and turns the sword on himself. Antony then falls on his sword, but fails to kill himself outright. Decretas and the guard enter, but refuse to kill him. Decretas takes Antony's sword with the intention of currying favour with Caesar. A messenger then tells Antony the truth about Cleopatra. He gives orders that he be conveyed to the monument.

COMMENTARY

The mistaken thought that Cleopatra has thrown in her lot with Caesar unhinges Antony: 'Here I am Antony, / Yet cannot hold this visible shape' (lines 13–4). Then the thought of her suicide disarms him further: 'The sevenfold shield of Ajax cannot keep / This battery from my heart' (lines 38–9). The suicide of the loyal Eros raises sympathy for Antony, who can inspire such devotion, and is contrasted with the calculated prudence of Decretas in taking Antony's sword. With his life of a soldier at an end, 'No more a soldier' (line 42), Antony becomes like a 'bridegroom' in his death and runs to it 'As to a lover's bed' (lines 100–1) with no subsequent reproach when he finds that Cleopatra has deceived him.

 QUESTION
The audience's knowledge that the report of Cleopatra's suicide is a ruse makes this scene one of intense dramatic irony that emphasises Antony's delusion. Is the audience's involvement in Antony's fate thereby enhanced or diminished?

GLOSSARY	
2	**dragonish** shaped like a dragon
3	**vapour** mist or cloud
8	**black vesper's pageants** the deceptive shows that approaching night puts on
10	**The rack dislimns** the cloud wipes out
12	**knave** boy, or servant
19–20	**Packed cards … triumph** cheated in dealing the cards and treacherously allowed him to trump my glory; wordplay on 'triumph', which can mean a victory and the official parade celebrating it, but also a trump card
23	**She has robbed me of my sword** compare with Cleopatra's own boast that she has worn Antony's 'sword Philippan' (II.5.23). The Roman point of view is consistently that Antony has allowed himself to be unmanned by Cleopatra
38	**The sevenfold shield of Ajax** Ajax, a stout defender, had a shield made of brass lined with seven layers of oxhide
39	**battery** bombardment, a military metaphor
40	**thy continent** your body (which contains the heart)
42	**Bruisèd pieces** referring primarily to the armour that he is taking off, but also to his emotional bruising
49	**Seal** finish
50	**Eros! – I come, my queen – Eros!** in classical mythology, Eros is the god of love
53	**Dido and her Aeneas** mythical lovers, not actually united after death, since Dido did not forgive Aeneas for deserting her to go and found Rome. Is this Shakespeare's mistake or Antony's? It is characteristic of the desire of the protagonists to see themselves in grand mythical terms
58	**Quartered** divided up *continued*

GLOSSARY

63	**exigent** final emergency
65	**Th'inevitable prosecution** the unavoidable pursuit
72	**windowed** placed as in a window
73	**with pleached arms** with hands bound behind him
75	**wheeled seat** chariot
98	**brave instruction** courageous example
98–9	**got upon me / A nobleness in record** have beaten me in winning a noble place in history

SCENE 15

- Antony dies in Cleopatra's arms.

CHECK THE BOOK

Roman greatness was a general theme in the Renaissance. For Shakespeare's imaginative engagement with Rome and Roman values generally and in this play, see Robert S. Miola, *Shakespeare's Rome* (CUP, 1983).

Antony is brought to the monument. Cleopatra will not come down because she fears that she will be captured. Thus he has to be hoisted up. Antony, selfless in death and concerned for her safety, bids her trust no one about Caesar but Proculeius. Cleopatra replies that she will put her trust in her own hands. Antony pronounces his own epitaph: 'a Roman, by a Roman / Valiantly vanquished' (lines 57–8). On his death Cleopatra faints, then movingly laments his passing.

COMMENTARY

This scene is discussed in **Extended commentaries**.

GLOSSARY

14	**Not Caesar's valour** Antony's valour has triumphed by virtue of his suicide, regarded as an act of self-control by the Romans
24	**full-fortuned** victorious, favoured by fortune, lucky
25	**Be brooched with me** be ornamented with me
29	**Demuring** looking at me demurely; the picture of Octavia is that of the dignified and sober, if slightly complacent, Roman matron
32	**Here's sport indeed!** Cleopatra is being ironic
33	**heaviness** literally weight, and also meaning grief

GLOSSARY	
34	Juno wife of Jove, the most powerful of the classical goddesses
35	Mercury the messenger of the gods
65	The soldier's pole perhaps the polestar, a standard, or a maypole
74	chares chores
78	sottish stupid
84	Good sirs addressed to her women

ACT V

SCENE 1

- Caesar hears of Antony's death.
- Caesar assures an Egyptian messenger of his goodwill towards Cleopatra.

Decretas enters Caesar's camp with news of Antony's suicide. Caesar weeps and pays him tribute. His tribute is interrupted by the arrival of a messenger from Cleopatra seeking to know his intentions. Caesar courteously reassures him that she will be treated honourably. After he has departed, he gives instructions to Proculeius to allay her fears, lest she kill herself and deprive him of her part in his Roman triumph. He sends Gallus after him.

COMMENTARY

The words of Decretas and the tribute of Caesar continue to uphold the dignity of Antony even if the tone is less exalted. Decretas is, after all, changing sides, and Maecenas perceptively remarks that Caesar's tears are the consequence of seeing his own fate potentially mirrored in that of Antony. In command and efficient as ever, Caesar is not so overcome by the news that he allows feelings of sorrow (or triumph) to interfere with the business of the moment, so that the interrupting messenger is dealt with straight away. Once again his response is above all political: he will do anything to

CONTEXT

When Caesar, in **hyperbolic** language, suggests that Antony's death should have produced prodigious effects – 'shook lions into civil streets' (line 16) – the Jacobean audience would doubtless have recalled the prodigies that were supposed to have followed the death of Julius Caesar. This play, like the earlier *Julius Caesar*, incorporates elements of the supernatural (such as the soothsayer) that were a feature of dramatic productions of the time.

CONTEXT

It was customary
for a successful
Roman general
to be awarded
an official triumph
by the senate
in which he
processed through
the city to the
temple of Jupiter
on the Capitol and
paraded captives
taken in the course
of a military
campaign.

ensure that Cleopatra survives to grace his triumphant return to Rome. The audience is never unsure about his motives, even if Cleopatra has to guess at them.

GLOSSARY

9	**his haters** those who hate him
18	**doom** death
19	**moiety** half
27	**The gods rebuke me** because he is shedding tears
36	**launch** lance
39	**stall** live
43	**In top of all design** in worthiest enterprise
49	**meeter season** more appropriate time
54	**intents** intentions
57	**by some of ours** through some of our representatives
63	**quality of her passion** the nature of her grief
65–6	**her life in Rome … triumph** her presence in Rome at my triumph would immortalise it
74	**hardly** reluctantly

SCENE 2

- Cleopatra commits suicide to defeat Caesar and join Antony.

This long scene may be regarded as having three movements. In the first Cleopatra explores Caesar's intentions towards her and comes to suspect what they are. In the second, through gaining Dolabella's sympathy, she becomes more certain in her knowledge; there is nothing in her meeting with Caesar to make her think otherwise and on Caesar's departure Dolabella is even more specific. In the third she acts to defeat these intentions.

LINES 1–62

Cleopatra enters with her thoughts on suicide. Proculeius then enters with reassuring words; if she accepts his authority, Caesar will take heed of her wishes. Cleopatra hopes for her kingdom, or, failing that, for her son to inherit, and agrees to meet him. Gallus enters and disarms her of the dagger that she draws. Her compliant attitude changes after his intervention.

Gallus bids Proculeius guard her. In ambiguous words the latter begs her not to 'abuse my master's bounty by / Th'undoing of yourself. Let the world see / His nobleness well acted' (lines 43–5). Proculeius doubtless means Cleopatra to understand that Caesar is concerned that his reputation for clemency and magnanimity will be harmed by her suicide. She rightly suspects another meaning: that Caesar wishes to keep her alive so that he can make a theatrical spectacle of her in a glorious Roman triumph, a fate that the queen judges to be worse than death.

COMMENTARY

At the beginning of the scene Cleopatra seems resolved on suicide. Misfortune, she says, gives her a better perspective on life, a Stoic perspective in which the individual despises the gifts of fortune and triumphs over bad fortune by virtue of inner strength and resolution. However, in what follows, she seems also to be trying to establish exactly what Caesar's intentions are. In answer to Proculeius's question about what she demands of Caesar, she replies that 'majesty, to keep decorum, must / No less beg than a kingdom' (lines 17–8). Is she playing for time, or genuinely seeking to see if she can survive intact? Cleopatra's attempt with the dagger may be interpreted as an impulsive instinct when cornered; it is not clear whether it is directed against her captors or against herself. What is clear throughout this scene (as at the moment of Antony's death at IV.15.27–9) is her proud fear of humiliation as she contemplates being paraded in Rome and before the judging eye of Octavia.

QUESTION
Does Cleopatra die principally to be with Antony or to defeat Caesar?

GLOSSARY	
3	**knave** servant
5	**that thing** suicide
7	**palates more the dung** tastes again the base product of earth (dung) which nourishes the poorest and the most powerful
24	**grace** goodwill
26	**sweet dependency** willing submission to his authority
	continued

GLOSSARY	
29	**his fortune's vassal** the servant of his success; she acknowledges his authority
42	**rids our dogs of languish** puts an end to the lingering diseases of dogs
48	**Worth many babes and beggars!** those to whom death most readily comes
53	**pinioned** with arms tied behind, or with clipped wings
56	**shouting varletry** the noisy common people
60	**Blow me into abhorring!** lay eggs upon me and make me repellent

LINES 62–110

Dolabella enters (at line 64) and takes over from Proculeius. Cleopatra tells Dolabella of her grandly imagined dream of Antony: 'His delights / Were dolphin-like', and so forth (lines 88–9). Dolabella is moved by her words and tells her what she desires to know: that Caesar intends to lead her in triumph through Rome.

COMMENTARY

Whatever evidence there may be that Cleopatra is preoccupied with her own safety, her remarkable dream of Antony provides contrary evidence of her grand passion grandly represented in her poetic imagining. When she says that 'It's past the size of dreaming' (line 97), she is literally saying that no mere dream could equal the reality. On the other hand her words suggest an awareness that the dream is but a dream and does not correspond to reality. She sets 'fancy' (line 98) above nature, but then continues: 'yet t'imagine / An Antony were nature's piece 'gainst fancy, / Condemning shadows quite' (lines 98–100). That is to say, an Antony such as she has imagined would be nature's masterpiece, a figure superior to anything merely imagined, entirely discrediting the shadowy figments of the imagination; in what is said about nature and fancy, this speech about Antony bears similarities with Enobarbus's speech about Cleopatra at II.2.196–223. Her transcendent poetic imagining here touches the sublime.

> **CONTEXT**
>
> In the imagining of Antony here there may be an allusion to the Colossus of Rhodes, a gigantic statue that was one of the Seven Wonders of the ancient world.

GLOSSARY	
75	**your trick** your habit
82	**bestrid** straddled
82–3	**his reared arm / Crested the world** his raised arm dominated the world
83–4	**propertied / As all the tunèd spheres** endowed with the heavenly music of the spheres
85	**quail** make quail or quake
88–90	**His delights ... lived in** just as dolphins show their backs above the water that is the element in which they live, so Antony rose above the pleasures that were his element
90	**In his livery** in his service
91	**crowns and crownets** kings and princes
92	**plates** coins

LINES 111–226

Caesar then enters (at line 111) and treats Cleopatra with diplomatic authority. She is dignified in offering her obeisance, handing him an account of her treasure and monies. She bids her treasurer, Seleucus, ratify its contents, but when he says that she has kept back as much as she has declared, she is greatly humiliated, though Caesar professes to admire her prudence in making provision for herself and allows her to keep her treasure, departing in peace. After he has left, Dolabella confirms Caesar's intention to take her to Rome.

COMMENTARY

There is an element of shadow-boxing in this encounter between Caesar and Cleopatra. We know of his intentions, so we can see his political manoeuvring when he seeks to exonerate Cleopatra at the expense of Antony. When Cleopatra acknowledges 'frailties which before / Have often shamed our sex' (lines 123–4) she may not be sincere, but it is significant that she does not seek to put the blame on Antony. It is not clear whether she keeps back some of her treasure because she wishes to fool Caesar into thinking that she wants to live, or whether she really does want to live.

After Caesar has gone, she shows that she has taken the measure of him, perceiving him to be all words, and her whispers to Charmian,

CHECK THE FILM
In the 1972 BBC film version of the play the ending is much less ambiguous. All reference to the treasure is cut; the interview with Caesar is shorter; and her final words to him, 'My master, and my lord!' (line 190), which could be interpreted as a seductive gesture (rejected by Caesar), are also cut.

CONTEXT

When Cleopatra imagines 'Some squeaking Cleopatra boy my greatness' (line 220), we are reminded that her part on the Jacobean stage was played by a boy actor.

to judge from Charmian's reply, concern arrangements to be made for her suicide. Dolabella enters and tells her of Caesar's arrangements: Caesar will journey through Syria; within three days she and her children will be sent on ahead.

GLOSSARY

119	**written in our flesh** shown in our war wounds
125	**enforce** emphasise
129	**lay on me a cruelty** make me look cruel in the eyes of the world; Caesar is concerned about what in the modern world would be called his image
131	**your children** in threatening these Caesar shows his true political colours
135	**scutcheons** shields showing coats of arms
138	**brief** summary list
151	**How pomp is followed!** how power (Caesar's) is courted
166	**Immoment toys** unimportant trivialities
173–4	**the cinders of my spirits / Through th'ashes of my chance** the living fire of my spirit which is concealed beneath my burnt-out fortunes; she does, in fact, show in this exchange some of her old fire
185	**Make not your thoughts your prisons** do not think you are a prisoner
192	**Be noble to myself** do the honourable thing, that is commit suicide
199	**my love makes religion to obey** my regard for you makes it a matter of duty to obey; Dolabella seems to have fallen under Cleopatra's spell
208	**puppet** as in a show; Cleopatra imagines being exhibited in an Egyptian tableau for the entertainment of the common people
209	**Mechanic** engaged in manual work, working class
212	**Rank of gross diet** smelling of bad food
214	**Saucy lictors** insolent (perhaps lascivious) officers of magistrates
215–16	**scald rhymers / Ballad us out o'tune** contemptible poets shall sing our story in ballads
217	**Extemporally** in impromptu performances

LINES 226–327

Convinced that she will become part of a Roman pageant, Cleopatra now determines to defeat Caesar's purposes, bidding Charmian fetch all her regalia for her final scene. A guardsman enters with a simple rustic character carrying a basket of figs, in which are concealed the asps whose poison will provide the means of release. Charmian returns with her regalia. Cleopatra dons her regal robes: 'Give me my robe; put on my crown; I have / Immortal longings in me' (lines 279–80). She bids farewell to her maids, who share her fate, and dies with Antony's name on her lips.

COMMENTARY

Fully sure of Caesar's intentions to make a vulgar theatrical exhibition of her in his Roman triumph, Cleopatra contrives her own regal pageant by which she will defeat his purposes and retain her dignity; her death is, in fact, accompanied by the ceremonial ritual associated with a coronation.

Lesser characters have their part to play in the grand climax; the clown, with his verbal fumbling and bawdy innuendo, injects a comic note (the incongruity of which only serves to heighten tension), while her maidservants in their loyalty and affection help both to give a human touch and to exalt Cleopatra in Charmian's touching tribute as a 'lass unparalleled' (line 315).

CHECK THE BOOK

Nowhere in the play is its mixed character more vividly apparent than in the semi-humorous exchange between Cleopatra and the simple countryman as the moment of intense climax approaches. Like the English history plays (especially those featuring Falstaff), *Antony and Cleopatra* contains a significant amount of comedy. For a discussion of its generic mix, see Barbara C. Vincent, '*Antony and Cleopatra* and the Rise of Comedy' in *Antony and Cleopatra* (New Casebooks, 1994), edited by John Drakakis.

GLOSSARY	
228	**Cydnus** the river down which she had sailed in her barge when first she met Antony
240	**marble-constant** as unchanging as marble
	the fleeting moon the moon as it waxes and wanes is a symbol of inconstancy. Earlier Cleopatra had appeared in the costume of the Egyptian moon goddess, Isis, at III.6.16–9
243	**worm of Nilus** the snake of the Nile, the asp
247	**immortal** the clown means mortal
252	**given to lie** to tell a lie, or to lie with men
257	**falliable** he means infallible
280	**Immortal longings** longs for immortality
282	**yare** quick
288	**other elements** earth and water continued

GLOSSARY

292	**aspic** the poison of the asp
300	**curlèd Antony** carefully barbered. When they first met, Antony was 'barbered ten times o'er' (II.2.229)
303	**intrinsicate** mysteriously intricate
305	**dispatch** end it quickly
306–7	**ass / Unpolicied** a fool outwitted in his policy
315	**Downy windows** eyelids as soft as down
317	**awry** crooked

LINES 328–64

Caesar and his train enter (at line 331) to discover that Cleopatra has defeated their purposes. Caesar pronounces a eulogy on Cleopatra and Antony.

COMMENTARY

CHECK THE FILM

Caesar's last words talk of Roman ceremony but the final image in the 1972 BBC film is of the regal Cleopatra, ceremonially crowned and majestic in death. This is surely a true visual representation of the audience's final impression. The film reflects the reality of the Jacobean stage by not having elaborate settings, but very effective use is made of costumes to suggest Egyptian splendour and luxury.

Caesar's magnanimity in his reaction to Cleopatra's death, which has defeated his purposes, recalls that of Mark Antony in Shakespeare's earlier play *Julius Caesar* on hearing of the death of Brutus, when he speaks the final words of the play in praise of the enemy he has just defeated in battle. His final speech with its solemn and dignified rhetoric sets the seal upon the lovers' story, which will be celebrated for ever after. At the same time it is by no means out of character, for he preserves for himself a measure of glory in their end. The speech can be said to serve his purposes after the high Roman fashion.

GLOSSARY

329	**Touch their effects** reach their expected results
334	**She levelled at our purposes** she guessed our intentions
346	**In her strong toil of grace** in the powerful snare of her beauty
347	**something blown** something swollen
357	**clip** embrace
364	**solemnity** ceremonious occasion

EXTENDED COMMENTARIES

TEXT 1 – II.2.196–250

Antony, having returned to Rome to meet his fellow triumvirs to deal with the threat posed by Pompey, has just agreed to marry Octavia, Caesar's sister. The triumvirs have left the stage and Enobarbus is telling Maecenas and Agrippa, Caesar's followers, about life in Egypt. The subject soon turns to Cleopatra and her first meeting with Antony. This famous passage is based quite closely upon the description that Shakespeare read in North's Plutarch (see **Further reading**). Comparison with North's prose will serve to throw into distinct relief certain characteristics of Shakespeare's poetic technique here and throughout the play.

(The italicised words mark material common to both North and Shakespeare. The passage in North can be found on pp. 214–15 of The New Penguin Shakespeare.)

ENOBARBUS
    The *barge* she sat in, like a burnished throne,
    Burned on the water. The *poop* was beaten *gold*;
    Purple the *sails*, and so perfumèd that
    The winds were lovesick with them. The *oars* were *silver*,
    Which to the tune of *flutes kept stroke* and made   200
    The water which they beat to follow faster,
    As amorous of their strokes. For her own *person*,
    It beggared all description. She did lie
    In her *pavilion*, *cloth-of-gold* of *tissue*,
    O'erpicturing that *Venus* where we see   205
    The fancy outwork nature. On each side her
    Stood *pretty* dimpled *boys*, like smiling *cupids*,
    With divers-coloured *fans*, whose wind did seem
    To glow the delicate cheeks which they did cool,
    And what they undid did.

AGRIPPA   O, rare for Antony!   210

ENOBARBUS
    Her *gentlewomen*, like the *Nereides*,
    So many *mermaids*, tended her i'th'eyes,
    And made their bends adornings. At the *helm*

QUESTION
This is a descriptive passage of high and entrancing poetry. It is almost as if Cleopatra has cast a spell over everyone. There can only be a disparity between illusion and reality. What actress can live up to the glamorised and bewitching picture of Cleopatra it creates? More pertinently, what boy actor (since women's parts were played by boys in the theatre of Shakespeare's time) could credibly represent a character of such allure?

CONTEXT
This picture draws on the classical idea of beauty in which art perfects nature by eliminating her impurities. The artist creates a beautiful face by a combination of beautiful features that could scarcely be found in actuality, in which there is always some mark of imperfection.

A seeming mermaid steers. The silken *tackle*
Swell with the touches of those flower-soft hands,　　　　215
That yarely frame the office. From the barge
A strange invisible *perfume* hits the sense
Of the adjacent *wharfs*. The city cast
Her people out upon her; and Antony,
Enthroned i'th'*market-place*, did sit *alone*,　　　　　220
Whistling to th'air; which, but for vacancy,
Had gone to gaze on Cleopatra too,
And made a gap in nature.

AGRIPPA　　　　　　　　　　　Rare Egyptian!

ENOBARBUS
　Upon her landing, Antony *sent* to her,
　Invited her to *supper*. She replied　　　　　　　225
　It should be better he became her guest;
　Which she entreated. Our courteous Antony,
　Whom ne'er the word of 'No' woman heard speak,
　Being barbered ten times o'er, goes to the feast,
　And, for his ordinary, pays his heart　　　　　　230
　For what his eyes eat only.

AGRIPPA　　　　　　　　　　　Royal wench!
　She made great Caesar lay his sword to bed.
　He ploughed her, and she cropped.

ENOBARBUS　　　　　　　　　　　I saw her once
　Hop forty paces through the public street;
　And, having lost her breath, she spoke, and panted,　　235
　That she did make defect perfection,
　And, breathless, power breathe forth.

MAECENAS
　Now Antony must leave her utterly.

ENOBARBUS
　Never; he will not.
　Age cannot wither her, nor custom stale　　　　　　240
　Her infinite variety. Other women cloy
　The appetites they feed, but she makes hungry
　Where most she satisfies; for vilest things

Become themselves in her, that the holy priests
Bless her when she is riggish.   245

MAECENAS
If beauty, wisdom, modesty, can settle
The heart of Antony, Octavia is
A blessèd lottery to him.

AGRIPPA   Let us go.
Good Enobarbus, make yourself my guest
Whilst you abide here.

ENOBARBUS   Humbly, sir, I thank you.   250
Exeunt

And now North's text:

Therefore when she was sent unto by divers letters, both from
Antonius himself and also from his friends, she made so light of
it and mocked Antonius so much that she disdained to set
forward otherwise but to take her *barge* in the river of Cydnus,
the *poop* whereof was of *gold*, the *sails* of *purple*, and the *oars* of
silver, which *kept stroke* in rowing after the sound of the music
of *flutes*, howboys, citherns, viols, and such other instruments as
they played upon in the barge. And now for the *person* of herself:
she was laid under a *pavilion of cloth-of-gold of tissue*, apparelled
and attired like the goddess *Venus* commonly drawn in *picture*;
and hard by her, on either hand of her, *pretty* fair *boys* apparelled
as painters do set forth god *Cupid*, with little *fans* in their hands,
with the which they fanned *wind* upon her. Her ladies and
gentlewomen also, the fairest of them were apparelled like the
nymphs *Nereides* (which are the *mermaids* of the waters) and
like the Graces, some steering the helm, others tending the *tackle*
and ropes of the *barge*, out of the which there came a wonderful
passing sweet savour of *perfumes*, that perfumed the *wharf's* side,
pestered with innumerable multitudes of people. Some of them
followed the barge all alongst the river's side; others also ran out
of the city to see her coming in; so that in the end there ran such
multitudes of people one after another to see her that *Antonius*

CONTEXT

North's prose is not
a direct translation
of the Greek of
Plutarch but is
from a French
version by Jacques
Amyot made in
1539. Amyot
probably
translated from a
literal Latin version
of the Greek rather
than directly from
the original.
North's prose is
not stilted and
scholarly; through
the detailed
descriptions the
entire scene is
vividly rooted in
recognisable
physical reality;
for example
the musical
instruments are
those of the
Elizabethan world.

was left post-*alone in the market-place* in his imperial seat to give audience. And there went a rumour in the people's mouths that the goddess Venus was come to play with the god Bacchus, for the general good of all Asia.

When Cleopatra *landed, Antonius sent to invite her to supper* to him. But she sent him word again, he should do *better* rather to come and sup with her. Antonius therefore, to show himself *courteous* unto her at her arrival, was contented to obey her, and went to supper to her; where he found such passing sumptuous fare, that no tongue can express it.

(Quoted in T. J. B. Spencer, ed., *Shakespeare's Plutarch*, Penguin Books, 1964, pp. 200–2)

In the structure and order of his description and in the incidents described Shakespeare follows North closely. Many of the actual words used in the description are the same. North's description in itself is arresting and appeals strongly to the imagination. Yet in comparison with Shakespeare it seems prosaic, not merely because it is prose with a greater diffuseness, but because it is so much less figurative. It is not true to say that North is not figurative at all. There are three striking similes at the heart of his description which together make the whole scene into an artistic tableau: Cleopatra is likened to Venus, the goddess of love; the pretty boys are like Cupid; and her gentlewomen are like Nereides, sea nymphs, daughters of the sea god Nereus.

Shakespeare has retained North's basic conception, but has composed his tableau with greater artistry. In each of his versions of the three comparisons he has amplified North and gone one better. The first of these comparisons in which Cleopatra is likened to Venus provides the key to Shakespeare's method here, to the working of his imagination in this passage.

Cleopatra's person is imagined as 'O'erpicturing that Venus where we see / The fancy outwork nature' (lines 205–6). Three orders of reality are implied here. There is nature, in the sense of beautiful women we know in the real world. Then there is art, through which the imagination of the artist, the 'fancy', is able to go one better by ironing out the imperfections of nature so that the beauty of the

CONTEXT

In Renaissance literary theory and practice, previous literature was considered to be public property, available to all for reworking, adaptation and excelling. Here the **hyperboles** and the **paradoxes** can illustrate the working of the doctrine of emulation at its best, as the poet excels his original source material against all expectation.

resulting picture perfects nature, giving us a classic Venus. Thirdly there is Cleopatra transcending even the classic Venus of the artist's imagination. Her beauty is thereby made to seem almost supernatural. This might be an absurd exaggeration if we had not already been prepared for something like this in the description that has gone before.

There are three striking figures, not mentioned in North, in the opening description. The barge, in a straightforward simile, is 'like a burnished throne' (line 196), that is, a gilt throne, suggesting majesty; 'Burned on the water' (line 197) is a daring metaphor, paradoxical in its mingling of the opposing elements of water and fire. Secondly, the sails are so perfumed that the winds are 'lovesick' (line 199) with them. Thirdly, the oars make the waves behind them follow faster, 'As amorous of their strokes' (line 202), another striking metaphor. The winds and the waves are courting the barge. Shakespeare's imagination, his 'fancy', is working with the raw material of North and animating its elements with a series of poetic figures. This animation not only heightens the realism of North's prose, but also brings an erotic suggestiveness.

The strange beauty of the scene is mirrored in the action of the boys' fans, which have the paradoxical effect of seeming to make the cheeks glow which they are cooling. In glowing cheeks a gentle eroticism is delicately continued. Here Shakespeare has taken an imaginative idea from North (likening the boys to Cupids), amplified it and integrated it more closely into his overall vision of an exotic strangeness. The gentlewomen are described in terms that Shakespeare found in North. But once again the poet has integrated them into the scene much more effectively by making them subordinate to Cleopatra, describing how they watch every movement of her eyes and bow gracefully as they attend to her wishes. The queen's imperiousness is enhanced as she is the absolute centre of all attention.

Shakespeare also enhances the femininity of the scene in which the 'flower-soft hands' deftly handle the 'silken tackle' (lines 214–15). The perfume is sweet in North, but more intriguingly strange in Shakespeare; its action as it 'hits the sense / Of the adjacent wharfs' (lines 217–18) is much more arresting too. The whole passage, in

> **CONTEXT**
>
> The heightening here is in line with the idea of poetry expressed in Sir Philip Sidney's *Defence of Poesy* (1579–80): 'Nature never set forth the earth in so rich tapestry as diverse poets have done ... her world is brazen, the poets only deliver a golden.'

fact, in both the prose and the poetry, has a strong, sensuous appeal, but Shakespeare manages to hit the senses by virtue both of stronger and of more subtle figurative suggestiveness.

With the rumour that Venus has come to play with Bacchus, the god of wine and revelry, for the good of all Asia, the description of Cleopatra's journey in North ends on a grand note. Shakespeare's very different conclusion, however, is both more daring and more fitting, given what has gone before and given the theme of his play.

He follows North in having the city unpeopled and Antony left alone as everyone goes to see Cleopatra. This is extravagance enough, but Shakespeare makes us imagine the impossible; the very air would have gone to gaze upon her if it could have done so without creating a vacancy in nature. This is another exaggeration that verges on the absurd, but is not absurd because it grows naturally from the whole conception of the almost supernatural quality of Cleopatra's beauty and attractiveness. Like the wind and the water, the element of air pays court to the phenomenal beauty of the scene in which Cleopatra dominates, leaving poor Antony enthroned as befits his powerful status but, 'Whistling to th'air' (line 221), rendered subjectless by the greater magnetism of the strange power of Cleopatra's attractiveness.

After the landing, we come down to earth, so to speak. The picture of Antony's courtesy and his elaborate grooming contains an element of humour; here Shakespeare has departed from North. In North the dinner is extravagant; Shakespeare makes a joke using the word 'ordinary' (line 230), which is a public dinner but one that might be had in a tavern. The banquet itself is insignificant in comparison to what happens at it; Antony loses his heart, feasting his eyes on Cleopatra. By this stage Shakespeare has departed from his source.

Enobarbus follows with a less exotic description of Cleopatra hopping through the streets till she is breathless. In the scene as a whole it is something of a paradox, coming after the regal majesty of her presence and progress on her barge. It contains within itself a paradox when she is said to 'make defect perfection' (line 236). What would be unbecoming in others is part of her completeness.

This prepares us for the greater paradoxes of her 'infinite variety' (line 241), where she is contrasted with other women in making hungry where most she satisfies: vile things in her are becoming and priests bless her when she is wanton.

The conception of her character therefore is grounded upon a paradoxical union of opposites. In itself this conception, which may be implicit in his source but is essentially Shakespeare's own, might not necessarily be convincing. What makes it convincing is the way that it is embodied and embedded in the language. The paradoxes are strongest at the end, but they are present in the extravagant language that evokes her mysterious beauty at the opening. The exaggerated language here, the use of hyperbole, is also present at the end: the idea that not just priests but holy priests, conscientious men of the cloth, bless her, whether literally or figuratively, when she is behaving like a harlot would be quite absurd if it was not wholly consistent with her spellbinding rarity, as established previously.

It would be wrong, however, to think of this scene solely as a more poetic version of the descriptive narrative account that we find in North's English version of Roman history. For this is drama and the dramatic dimension is crucial to its effect. Enobarbus has already been established in the audience's mind as a witty character who has a sharp-eyed appreciation of Cleopatra (Act I Scene 2). The full paradox of his picture of the enchanting harlot queen is brought out in conversation with his fellow Romans.

> **CONTEXT**
>
> Here and throughout this passage is that 'happy valiancy' by which the language of *Antony and Cleopatra* is distinguished in the phrase of the Romantic critic and poet Samuel Taylor Coleridge (1772–1834).

The interventions of Agrippa do not merely break up what would otherwise be a very long account; they add an appreciative dimension and they propel it forward. Agrippa is a hardbitten Roman soldier; that he should respond to the magnetism of what he is hearing re-enacts its original effect upon Antony. Given that 'Egyptian' was, in Shakespeare's day, synonymous with 'gypsy', there may be an **oxymoron** in 'Rare Egyptian!' (line 223). There certainly is an oxymoron in 'Royal wench!' (line 231), where 'wench' is a word of low status with possible suggestions of lasciviousness.

There is a grand wordplay in Agrippa's line: 'She made great Caesar lay his sword to bed' (line 232, referring to Julius Caesar); this wittily reinforces the idea of Cleopatra's indomitable sexual power, for she has caused the most powerful man in the world to sheath his sword. That is, in political and military terms, not to kill or conquer her, and in sexual terms the sword can be understood to have obvious phallic associations in view of the ploughing and cropping of the next line (referring to sexual intercourse and the subsequent birth of Caesarion). This interjection has the effect of moving Enobarbus's account towards the more earthy aspects of Cleopatra. Indeed the whole scene is skilfully orchestrated, starting with the mysterious eroticism of the scene on the water, coming down to earth with the landing and descending finally to the word 'riggish' (line 245).

CHECK THE NET
This passage is discussed by Norman N. Holland in '"The Barge She Sat In": Psychoanalysis and Syntactic Choices' at Mr William Shakespeare and the Internet: http://shakespeare.palomar.edu. This site contains other essays and material on the play.

The intervention of Maecenas, towards the end of the scene, calls to mind the political imperative of the moment when he says that Antony must sever the link. After all that Enobarbus has said we are inclined to believe him when he says that Antony cannot do so. Finally, when Maecenas hails the 'beauty, wisdom, modesty' of Octavia (line 246), starkly juxtaposed with the wantonness of Cleopatra, he evokes the alternative world that Antony has apparently embraced in agreeing to marry Octavia. Modesty is a well-chosen word. In relations between the sexes it suggest chastity; in general behaviour it suggests humility, freedom from excess and self-control. Is it likely that Antony, who has been susceptible to Cleopatra and who has already shown evidence of passion and excess, can ever be content with the modest Octavia? This is the question with which we are left at the end.

The qualities of this extract are thrown into even clearer relief if it is juxtaposed with the description of the same journey put into the mouth of Antony by John Dryden (1631–1700) in his neoclassical play featuring Antony and Cleopatra, *All for Love, or The World Well Lost* (1677):

CONTEXT
This play supplanted Shakespeare's in the eighteenth century and beyond (see **Critical history: Early responses**).

ANTONY
  Her galley down the silver Cydnos rowed,
  The tackling silk, the streamers waved with gold;
  The gentle winds were lodged in purple sails;
  Her nymphs, like Nereids, round her couch were placed,   165
  Where she, another sea-born Venus, lay.

DOLABELLA
No more; I would not hear it.

ANTONY   Oh, you must!
She lay, and leant her cheek upon her hand,
And cast a look so languishingly sweet
As if, secure of all beholders' hearts,   170
Neglecting she could take 'em. Boys like Cupids
Stood fanning with their painted wings the winds
That played about her face; but if she smiled,
A darting glory seemed to blaze abroad,
That men's desiring eyes were never wearied,   175
But hung upon the object. To soft flutes
The silver oars kept time; and while they played,
The hearing gave new pleasure to the sight,
And both to thought. 'Twas Heaven, or somewhat more;
For so she charmed all hearts, that gazing crowds   180
Stood panting on the shore, and wanted breath
To give their welcome voice.
                (John Dryden, *All for Love, or The World Well Lost*,
                Act III, lines 162–82, New Mermaids, 1975)

The elements of North and his artistic tableau are still visible, but the supernatural strangeness and exotic appeal that we find in Shakespeare have evaporated along with all that created them: his conceits, paradoxes and daring hyperboles. Can we imagine Shakespeare's Cleopatra casting a look so languishingly sweet? That the sound of the flutes should provide food for 'thought' is a limiting response. In Shakespeare the picture hits the senses so that we are ravished beyond mere thinking about it. Dryden's verse is smooth and elegant (more so than Shakespeare's), but the effect is tame.

TEXT 2 – II.5.1–66

After the triumvirs have settled their differences and Antony has agreed to marry Octavia, they depart. The scene now shifts to Alexandria, by which time Antony has made the marriage, unbeknown to Cleopatra.

> **CONTEXT**
> After the Restoration in the second half of the seventeenth century, there was a general reaction against what was perceived to be the irregularity and extravagance of the language and literature of the Elizabethan and Jacobean ages.

CLEOPATRA

Give me some music – music, moody food
Of us that trade in love.

ALL The music, ho!

Enter Mardian the eunuch

CLEOPATRA

Let it alone! Let's to billiards. Come, Charmian.

CHARMIAN

My arm is sore; best play with Mardian.

CLEOPATRA

As well a woman with an eunuch played 5
As with a woman. Come, you'll play with me, sir?

MARDIAN

As well as I can, madam.

CLEOPATRA

And when good will is showed, though't come too short,
The actor may plead pardon. I'll none now.
Give me mine angle. We'll to th'river; there, 10
My music playing far off, I will betray
Tawny-finned fishes. My bended hook shall pierce
Their slimy jaws; and as I draw them up,
I'll think them every one an Antony,
And say 'Ah, ha! Y'are caught!'

CHARMIAN 'Twas merry when 15
You wagered on your angling; when your diver
Did hang a salt fish on his hook, which he
With fervency drew up.

CLEOPATRA That time – O times! –
I laughed him out of patience; and that night
I laughed him into patience; and next morn, 20
Ere the ninth hour, I drunk him to his bed;
Then put my tires and mantles on him, whilst

> **CONTEXT**
> There is a notable **anachronism** at the opening of this scene when Cleopatra says 'Let's to billiards' (line 3), a reference to a game not invented till Shakespeare's time. Generally speaking, Shakespeare is careful to maintain the historical atmosphere, though never pedantically so.

I wore his sword Philippan.

    Enter a Messenger

              O, from Italy!
Ram thou thy fruitful tidings in mine ears,
That long time have been barren.

MESSENGER   Madam, madam –   25

CLEOPATRA
Antonio's dead! If thou say so, villain,
Thou kill'st thy mistress; but well and free,
If thou so yield him, there is gold and here
My bluest veins to kiss, a hand that kings
Have lipped, and trembled kissing.   30

MESSENGER
First, madam, he is well.

CLEOPATRA   Why, there's more gold.
But, sirrah, mark, we use
To say the dead are well. Bring it to that,
The gold I give thee will I melt and pour
Down thy ill-uttering throat.   35

MESSENGER
Good madam, hear me.

CLEOPATRA   Well, go to, I will.
But there's no goodness in thy face, if Antony
Be free and healthful; so tart a favour
To trumpet such good tidings? If not well,
Thou shouldst come like a Fury crowned with snakes,   40
Not like a formal man.

MESSENGER   Will't please you hear me?

CLEOPATRA
I have a mind to strike thee ere thou speak'st.
Yet, if thou say Antony lives, is well,
Or friends with Caesar, or not captive to him,
I'll set thee in a shower of gold, and hail   45
Rich pearls upon thee.

> **CONTEXT**
>
> The sword which Antony had used in the battle in which he and Octavius Caesar had defeated Brutus and Cassius at Philippi. In an earlier scene Agrippa, referring to Cleopatra's previous conquest of Julius Caesar, says, 'She made great Caesar lay his sword to bed' (II.2.232). The sword here and elsewhere clearly has symbolic associations.

> **CONTEXT**
>
> In Greek mythology the Furies, goddesses who avenge domestic and familial wrongs, are conceived as having snakes wreathed in their hair.

MESSENGER	Madam, he's well.
CLEOPATRA	Well said.
MESSENGER	And friends with Caesar.
CLEOPATRA	Th'art an honest man.
MESSENGER	Caesar and he are greater friends than ever.
CLEOPATRA	Make thee a fortune from me.
MESSENGER	But yet, madam –

CLEOPATRA
I do not like 'But yet'; it does allay   50
The good precedence. Fie upon 'But yet'!
'But yet' is as a gaoler to bring forth
Some monstrous malefactor. Prithee, friend,
Pour out the pack of matter to mine ear,
The good and bad together. He's friends with Caesar,   55
In state of health, thou sayst, and, thou sayst, free.

MESSENGER
Free, madam! No; I made no such report.
He's bound unto Octavia.

CLEOPATRA   For what good turn?

MESSENGER
For the best turn i'th'bed.

CLEOPATRA   I am pale, Charmian.

MESSENGER
Madam, he's married to Octavia.   60

CLEOPATRA
The most infectious pestilence upon thee!

She strikes him down

MESSENGER
Good madam, patience.

CLEOPATRA   What say you?

She strikes him

                    Hence,
Horrible villain, or I'll spurn thine eyes
Like balls before me! I'll unhair thy head!

She hales him up and down

Thou shalt be whipped with wire and stewed in brine,   65
Smarting in lingering pickle!

Though striking messengers is doubtless highly reprehensible behaviour (and drawing a knife on them, as Cleopatra does at the end of this scene, certainly is), this is a richly comic scene and a welcome change after the political manoeuvring in Rome. At the opening, missing Antony, Cleopatra is bored. Although we are always conscious of her regal status, we never see her engaged in matters of serious statecraft in the first part of the drama. Egypt is here the playful setting for music, games, sex talk and mirth.

To begin with the humour is at the expense of Mardian, the eunuch. There is bawdy innuendo, in which Mardian himself takes part, about the eunuch's inability to play properly with a woman sexually. Playing with Mardian then ceases to be an attractive proposition. Cleopatra's whim turns towards fishing. The humour now is at the expense of Antony. She will imagine every fish she catches to be Antony. The imagery here supports the notion that Antony is wholly entangled by the wily Cleopatra, who has her hooks in him, so to speak. Charmian reminds her of the time she played a trick on Antony by fixing a salted fish to his line which he then drew in with verve and enthusiasm as if it had been his own catch. Once again, Cleopatra is dominant, mocking and playing tricks upon her lover. More tricks follow when she recalls dressing him up in her clothes, while she wears his 'sword Philippan' (line 23). In this reversal of the usual roles, which had so scandalised Caesar when he heard report of it (I.4.5–7), she is again the dominant party, symbolically usurping the masculine role.

> **CONTEXT**
>
> 'Mood music' regularly featured in the theatrical performances of the time. Compare the famous opening of *Twelfth Night*: 'If music be the food of love, play on.'

The messenger enters with what the audience knows will be bad news for Cleopatra. Shakespeare uses dramatic irony here, exploiting the audience's superior knowledge for comic effect. He spins the scene out by making it difficult for the poor messenger to get a word in edgeways. Cleopatra's opening – a forceful sexual innuendo – is quite startling: 'Ram thou thy fruitful tidings in mine ears, / That long time have been barren' (lines 24–5). The normal social inhibitions do not apply to Cleopatra.

Her grand extravagance is apparent in the melodrama of her first speech. In it she imagines the messenger announcing Antony's death and then, if he pronounces him well, promises gold and her 'bluest veins to kiss' – emphasising her blue-blooded regality – 'a hand that kings / Have lipped, and trembled kissing' (lines 29–30). She is revealed here in full confidence of her sexual power. The punishment she envisages for him (melting the gold and pouring it down his throat) if still he should pronounce Antony dead, is correspondingly extreme and grand, as are the images of the Fury, the shower of gold and the hail of pearls. Shakespeare has endowed her with a rich and fertile imagination. (Crassus, a member of the First Triumvirate, died at the hands of the Parthians by having molten gold poured into his mouth. A brutally ironic death, it reflected the Parthian view that he had come simply to steal their gold (see **Chronology**).)

CHECK THE BOOK

For a radical feminist 'gynocentric' reading of the play, see Mary Hamer, 'Reading *Antony and Cleopatra* through Irigaray's *Speculum*' in *Antony and Cleopatra*, edited by Nigel Wood (Open University Press, 1996).

The scene builds up tension and then releases it in a highly effective dramatic explosion. Cleopatra's long comment on 'But yet' (lines 49–56), which she rightly sees as 'a gaoler to bring forth / Some monstrous malefactor', prepares us and her for the worst. Her misunderstanding of the messenger's meaning in 'bound' (line 58) resulting in his joke 'the best turn i'th'bed' (line 59) intensifies the irony. When finally the messenger delivers his news simply and directly in one line, the suspense that has been mounting is finally over. Cleopatra's sudden invective matches in verbal terms her physical action and in its extremity befits her tempestuous character. The scene exhibits her dominance and shows her to be driven by strong and uncontrollable passions. It also shows us what Enobarbus has described in his picture of her: a character of apparent contradictions, queen, virago and fishwife, all somehow cohering in one linguistic creation.

TEXT 3 – IV.15.13–90

After Antony's bungled attempt at suicide, a messenger informs him
that Cleopatra, whom he believed to have committed suicide, is still
alive and has taken refuge in her monument. He gives orders that he
should be taken to her.

CLEOPATRA
    Help, friends below! Let's draw him hither.

ANTONY   Peace!
    Not Caesar's valour hath o'erthrown Antony,
    But Antony's hath triumphed on itself.   15

CLEOPATRA
    So it should be, that none but Antony
    Should conquer Antony, but woe 'tis so!

ANTONY
    I am dying, Egypt, dying; only
    I here importune death awhile, until
    Of many thousand kisses the poor last   20
    I lay upon thy lips.

CLEOPATRA   I dare not, dear;
    Dear my lord, pardon. I dare not,
    Lest I be taken. Not th'imperious show
    Of the full-fortuned Caesar ever shall
    Be brooched with me. If knife, drugs, serpents, have   25
    Edge, sting, or operation, I am safe.
    Your wife Octavia, with her modest eyes
    And still conclusion, shall acquire no honour
    Demuring upon me. But come, come, Antony –
    Help me, my women – we must draw thee up.   30
    Assist, good friends.

ANTONY   O, quick, or I am gone.

CLEOPATRA
    Here's sport indeed! How heavy weighs my lord!
    Our strength is all gone into heaviness,
    That makes the weight. Had I great Juno's power,
    The strong-winged Mercury should fetch thee up   35

> **CONTEXT**
> Cleopatra's position above Antony, who is hoisted up to her, presupposes two theatrical levels. Doubtless there was a balcony above the stage of the kind envisaged in the famous scene in *Romeo and Juliet*.

And set thee by Jove's side. Yet come a little;
Wishers were ever fools, O, come, come, come.

They heave Antony aloft to Cleopatra

And welcome, welcome! Die when thou hast lived;
Quicken with kissing. Had my lips that power,
Thus would I wear them out.

ALL THE GUARDS   A heavy sight!   40

ANTONY
    I am dying, Egypt, dying.
    Give me some wine, and let me speak a little.

CLEOPATRA
    No, let me speak, and let me rail so high
    That the false housewife Fortune break her wheel,
    Provoked by my offence.

ANTONY   One word, sweet queen.   45
    Of Caesar seek your honour, with your safety. O!

CLEOPATRA
    They do not go together.

ANTONY   Gentle, hear me:
    None about Caesar trust but Proculeius.

CLEOPATRA
    My resolution and my hands I'll trust,
    None about Caesar.   50

ANTONY
    The miserable change now at my end
    Lament nor sorrow at, but please your thoughts
    In feeding them with those my former fortunes,
    Wherein I lived; the greatest prince o'th'world,
    The noblest; and do now not basely die,   55
    Not cowardly put off my helmet to
    My countryman; a Roman, by a Roman
    Valiantly vanquished. Now my spirit is going;
    I can no more.

CONTEXT

Since later it proves
to be Dolabella not
Proculeius who
tells Cleopatra
the truth about
Caesar's intentions,
the advice given to
her by Antony on
his deathbed that
she trust no one
but Proculeius
is another bad
judgement on his
part.

CLEOPATRA   Noblest of men, woo't die?
Hast thou no care of me? Shall I abide   60
In this dull world, which in thy absence is
No better than a sty? O, see, my women,

                          Antony dies

The crown o'th'earth doth melt. My lord!
O, withered is the garland of the war,
The soldier's pole is fall'n; young boys and girls   65
Are level now with men. The odds is gone,
And there is nothing left remarkable
Beneath the visiting moon.

       She faints

CHARMIAN   O, quietness, lady!

IRAS
She's dead too, our sovereign.

CHARMIAN   Lady!

IRAS   Madam!

CHARMIAN
O madam, madam, madam!   70

IRAS
Royal Egypt! Empress!

CHARMIAN   Peace, peace, Iras!

CLEOPATRA
No more but e'en a woman, and commanded
By such poor passion as the maid that milks
And does the meanest chares. It were for me
To throw my sceptre at the injurious gods,   75
To tell them that this world did equal theirs
Till they had stolen our jewel. All's but naught.
Patience is sottish, and impatience does
Become a dog that's mad; then is it sin
To rush into the secret house of death   80
Ere death dare come to us? How do you, women?

> **CONTEXT**
>
> Commentators suggest that **'passion'** here probably refers not simply to passionate grief but to *hysterica passio*, a condition common to women, one of the symptoms of which was thought to be fainting. Cleopatra has just recovered from fainting here.

What, what, good cheer! Why, how now, Charmian?
My noble girls! Ah, women, women, look,
Our lamp is spent, it's out. Good sirs, take heart.
We'll bury him; and then, what's brave, what's noble,   85
Let's do't after the high Roman fashion,
And make death proud to take us. Come, away.
This case of that huge spirit now is cold.
Ah, women, women! Come; we have no friend
But resolution, and the briefest end.   90

Exeunt, bearing off Antony's body

In Antony's death scene, the presentation of the lovers confirms and consolidates the impression they have made throughout the play. What is new in the case of Antony is a touching concern for Cleopatra's safety and honour. Coming from the battlefield where he has just been defeated, although he desires to kiss her a final time, his first thoughts are almost entirely upon his own honour and reputation as a soldier. In a formal speech, he asks to be remembered for his former glory, concluding with the dignified assertion that he is 'a Roman, by a Roman / Valiantly vanquished' (lines 57–8).

It may be that he has in mind his defeat by Caesar. Perhaps it is more likely, given his earlier comment to Cleopatra that 'Not Caesar's valour hath o'erthrown Antony, / But Antony's hath triumphed on itself' (lines 14–15), that he is referring to the act of taking his own life. In the Roman world suicide was regarded as a noble act, as Cleopatra recognises at the end of the scene when she herself contemplates doing 'what's brave, what's noble … after the high Roman fashion' (lines 85–6). But in either meaning, though it is a noble phrase, it does not quite ring true; after his botched suicide and all that has led up to it, Antony is putting on a brave face and the best gloss possible on what is a sorry state of affairs.

CONTEXT

That suicide is to be inferred is confirmed later by Cleopatra's reference to Caesar as 'full-fortuned' (line 24). Caesar is repeated associated with 'fortune'. The Roman suicide is regarded as a means of triumphing over (mis)fortune.

Until Antony has actually died, Cleopatra's thoughts too are primarily on her own safety and honour. She will not risk coming down to him; he has to be brought up to her. (Some commentators have seen an echo here of the scene in which Cleopatra envisages drawing up Antony on a fish-hook.) Prominent in her mind is the thought that she might become an ornament ('Be brooched') in the triumphal spectacle ('th'imperious show') of the successful Caesar, where Octavia may gain 'honour', that is reputation and status, by an intolerable exercise of virtue at her expense (lines 23–9). Far from being absorbed in each other to the exclusion of all else, therefore, the lovers exhibit the intense self-regard that they have shown from the beginning.

Antony's sense of himself as a valiant, indeed triumphant, Roman is matched by the regal imperiousness of Cleopatra, reflected in many of the words and images used by her and those about her. She is sovereign – 'Royal Egypt!' (line 71) – and empress; she talks of a crown, her sceptre and a jewel. She associates herself with divinity when she wishes she had Juno's power to set Antony by Jove. Her grand extravagance is reflected in characteristic **hyperboles**: she would rail so strongly that Fortune might break her wheel; she would find it becoming to throw her sceptre against the gods that permit this harm and hurt.

> **CONTEXT**
>
> The image of the goddess Fortune with a wheel (by the turning of which she determines human fate) is traditional. Cleopatra both acknowledges her power and belittles her by associating her wheel with the spinning wheel of a housewife.

Yet the imperial note is only one of several sounded in her language in this scene: there is ironic awareness in 'Here's sport indeed!' (line 32), and in the wordplay on 'weighs' that follows, meaning both physical weight and the weight of grief, her smart verbal intelligence is harnessed to pathetic effect. Her sensuality, too, is evoked when she welcomes Antony with kisses, even if they cannot quicken him into life. Some commentators have seen sexual meaning in her use of the words 'die' and 'quicken' here (lines 38–9). If it is there, far from being unfitting, it maintains the consistency of her characterisation.

Before this extract Antony has been on stage for some time and we have been absorbed in his fate. But it is characteristic of the pattern of their relationship as Shakespeare has presented it that even his death should be upstaged by Cleopatra. As soon as Antony has died she takes centre stage and dominates the remainder of the play. Just as her real feelings for Antony are first seen after he has departed from Egypt ('O happy horse, to bear the weight of Antony!' I.5.21), so at the moment of his departure they come to the surface here. What is most moving is the **paradox** that her words both sustain the

CHECK THE BOOK

For a discussion of the death of Antony in the light of Plutarch's idea of the noble Roman which Shakespeare follows but varies, see Reuben A. Brower, *Hero and Saint: Shakespeare and the Graeco-Roman Heroic Tradition* (OUP, 1971); see also 'The question of the tragic', pp. 43–9, in the latest Arden Shakespeare edition, edited by John Wilders (1995).

image of Antony as a powerful military hero at line 64 ('O, withered is the garland of the war') while at the same time recognising that death obliterates all the distinctions by which they have lived their lives ('young boys and girls / Are level now with men', lines 65–6).

After Cleopatra has fainted, in what is perhaps her most human and moving moment in the play, she sees that this levelling effect applies to herself too: 'No more but e'en a woman' (line 72). Where Antony had been restrained and formal in his acceptance of the inevitable at the end, Cleopatra's final speech is characteristically varied in its emotional range and fluid in its movement. She humbly identifies with 'the maid that milks' at the beginning (line 73) then grandly with the gods themselves, whom she deigns to upbraid. She shifts again, in feeling that patience is for fools while to rail is madness. As her thoughts turn to death, they also look beyond herself to her maidservants. After the shifts and swings in mood and thought (what an opportunity for an accomplished actress), as she contemplates a way to 'make death proud to take us' (line 87), she reasserts her wavering sense of identity in the calm resolution (both courage and decision) of the close.

PART THREE

CRITICAL APPROACHES

THE STRUCTURE OF THE PLOT

The Folio text does not contain act divisions, but it does provide stage directions and indications of scene settings from which a reliable sequence can be established; act divisions were provided by Shakespeare's first editors in the eighteenth century. This early division of the play into acts and scenes has generally been accepted, though it should be noted that in the Oxford edition of *The Complete Works* (edited by Wells and Taylor, 1988) Agrippa's three-line utterance at the beginning of Act IV Scene 7 is counted as a separate scene, so that in this edition there are sixteen scenes in Act IV. The usual total of forty-two scenes is considerably more than in any other play by Shakespeare and tells us something of his technique in *Antony and Cleopatra*.

The play is marked by a distinct **antithetical** structure. In the first half before the movement towards Actium, there is the contrast between scenes in Egypt and the political scenes in which Roman business is conducted. Act I is set mostly in Egypt, with a contrasting scene in Caesar's house (Scene 4) in which Caesar expresses his disapproval of Antony's doings in Egypt; Act II, which covers the Roman business with Pompey, is interrupted by one scene in Egypt (Scene 5) in which Cleopatra beats the messenger who has come to tell her of Antony's marriage to Octavia. Act III opens with Ventidius on the plains of Syria, returns to Rome for the parting of the triumvirs, switches to Egypt to see Cleopatra asking about Octavia, then goes to Antony's house in Athens for two scenes of political business, returning to Rome for further political business as the triumvirate breaks up before moving to Actium for Scene 7.

Here at the halfway point the scene setting follows the logic of the action, moving between Actium and Cleopatra's palace in Alexandria. Where the antithesis before Actium has been between Egypt and Roman business (the private world of Antony and Cleopatra and the public world of Roman politics), after Actium the antithesis is between what is happening in Antony's camp and what is happening in Caesar's camp.

CHECK
THE BOOK
The introductory material in the latest Arden Shakespeare edition (1995), especially the sections on 'The question of unity', pp. 12–26, and 'The question of structure', pp. 26–38, and the section in The New Cambridge Shakespeare edition (1990) entitled 'Genre and structure', pp. 30–4, provide useful starting points. For a fuller treatment, see Janet Adelman, *The Common Liar: An Essay on Antony and Cleopatra* (Yale University Press, 1973).

The continual hurry of the action, the variety of incidents, and the quick succession of one personage after another, call the mind forward without intermission from the first act to the last. But the power of delighting is derived principally from the frequent changes of the scene.

(Quoted in *Johnson on Shakespeare*, edited by Walter Raleigh, OUP, 1908, p. 180)

To Samuel Johnson's verdict here, we may add that this juxtapositioning is a highly effective way of dramatising the split in Antony's public and private life and the consequences that this split entails in his conflict with Caesar. Thus the dramatic form or structure that Shakespeare has chosen reflects the major thematic concerns of the play.

To some extent this form is that of a chronicle play – a play that follows a broad sequence of events, often covering a long period of time (over ten years in the case of this play) in a straightforward chronological order. Yet this is not entirely true, because Shakespeare has begun in the middle of things, after Antony has got into political difficulties as a result of his affair with Cleopatra. Enobarbus's description of the lovers' first meeting (II.2.196–231) is a kind of retrospective narrative, though we hardly notice it as such. Similar is Caesar's praise of Antony's past exploits as a general. The point at which Shakespeare has chosen to begin indicates the main theme.

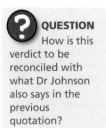

QUESTION
How is this verdict to be reconciled with what Dr Johnson also says in the previous quotation?

The structure of the play has not always been admired. Here is Samuel Johnson's verdict: 'The events, of which the principal are described according to history, are produced without any art of connection or care of disposition', p. 180. Close examination of the play in relation to that history (principally the account found in Plutarch's 'Life of Antony') reveals this verdict to be an exaggeration, to say the least.

In the first place there are omissions: for example, Antony's disastrous Parthian campaigns, in which it is estimated that he lost over thirty thousand troops, are not to Shakespeare's purpose; there are enough disasters without these. Antony's life with Octavia, which produced several children, is omitted. Then there are changes to the source ('care of disposition') and inventions. For example,

Cleopatra beats her treasurer, Seleucus, in Plutarch but the scene in which she beats the messenger who tells her of Antony's marriage to Octavia is an invention. Enobarbus is mentioned incidentally in Plutarch but the development of his character and role (see **Characterisation**) is a major Shakespearean invention which, among other things, gives coherence ('art of connection') to the plot.

Yet there are inherent difficulties in the chronicle approach. So much history has to be crammed into a short compass that there are gaps and omissions, omissions of things that, quite irrespective of any historical account, we may legitimately wish to know in the dramatisation of the events of the play. For example, when Antony promises Octavia that he will behave himself, is he at this moment sincere? (Consider that fewer than forty lines later he says that he has made the marriage for his peace and is leaving for the east in which his pleasure lies.) What was in Caesar's mind in allowing the one person he seems to care about to marry Antony? We have no way of knowing; the treatment of this stage of the story is quite superficial. Often we do not know as much as we might like to know about the motivation of the characters. Significantly, the play has few soliloquies, the place on the Renaissance stage where we might find motives explored and inner conflicts expressed.

QUESTION
The play is called a **tragedy** in the First Folio. Is there the depth of inner exploration that might be expected in a tragedy (especially when compared with the four great tragedies, *Hamlet*, *King Lear*, *Othello* and *Macbeth*)? If not, might it better be described more simply as a history play?

The broad sweep of the chronicle often precludes depth. But the fast-moving juxtaposition of scenes involving a vast number of characters compensates for any lack of depth by giving us complexity of a different sort; events are seen from a variety of perspectives to give us not simply a narrative sequence mostly from one point of view, as in Plutarch, but an active sense of history being made and destinies being determined from the interaction of competing forces, both personal and more broadly political. *Julius Caesar* centres upon the build up to, and consequences of, a single event (the assassination of Caesar). In contrast to this **unity** of action, in *Antony and Cleopatra* there is no particular dominant action but rather many events, both public and private, that follow on from what the Romans at the beginning of the play see as Antony's 'dotage'. The play derives what unity it has not from action or even from character but from this overarching theme.

CHARACTERISATION

The characterisations of Antony, Cleopatra and Octavius Caesar follow quite closely the portraits of them in Plutarch, except that Shakespeare has presented the lovers more attractively, while the opposite is true of Caesar. In Plutarch, though Antony is magnanimous, bountiful, courageous and convivial, he is also cruel, lecherous and corrupt. Shakespeare's Antony is far more noble. Cleopatra is perhaps surprisingly well presented in Plutarch as enchanting and exotic (see **Extended commentaries**) and also intelligent; the intense realisation of her as a paradoxical union of contradictory qualities is Shakespeare's own response to what he found in his source. Shakespeare has conceived Octavius very much as Antony's opposite; whereas in Plutarch he is said to have a weakness for women, in Shakespeare he is abstemious, censorious and cold. His political virtues are presented by the dramatist in such a way that they almost suggest a human limitation.

QUESTION

Shakespeare's Romans are significantly clarified in comparison with their originals in Plutarch; how then are we to account for the fact that his play produces an experience of greater complication, interest, penetration and depth than can be derived from a reading of Plutarch?

The principal characters are the subject of comment in the **Detailed summaries**, while the presentation of the lovers, particularly of Cleopatra, is discussed in detail in **Extended commentaries**. Shakespeare's dramatic construction and design are illustrated here with reference to what is Shakespeare's single most striking invention, his development of the character and role of Enobarbus.

The character of Antony's lieutenant Enobarbus contributes to the drama in a number of ways. Sympathetic to Antony from the start, his loyalty and fellow feeling help to establish the humanity of his captain in the course of the action. When at the beginning Antony says he wishes he had never met Cleopatra, instead of agreeing with him, Enobarbus offers the rejoinder that, had that been the case, Antony would have missed 'a wonderful / piece of work' (I.2.154–5). He does not share, therefore, the perspective of his fellow Roman soldiers Philo and Demetrius in the opening scene. In fact he is obviously enjoying life in Egypt and contributes to the relaxed humour of the Egyptian court, with appreciative comments, too, on Cleopatra.

When Antony says of Cleopatra, 'She is cunning past man's thought', **Enobarbus** disagrees: 'Alack, sir, no; her passions are made of / nothing but the finest part of pure love' (I.2.146–8). In their conversations at the beginning, and indeed in his role throughout, it is as if Enobarbus represents an ordinary reflection of something in Antony himself, as in a mirror. His wit and humour in response to the announcement of Fulvia's death – though eventually Antony silences him with 'No more light answers' (I.2.177) – anticipate the jovial side of Antony that will manifest itself in the galley scene.

Before the triumvirs meet, the diplomatic Lepidus tries to persuade Enobarbus to keep Antony calm and cool. Enobarbus will have none of it, saying he much prefers that Antony should speak his mind. He is forthright himself when he reminds Antony and Caesar that there will be time enough to quarrel after they have disposed of Pompey. To Antony's rebuke, 'Thou art a soldier only. Speak no more' (II.2.111), he boldly replies, 'That truth should be silent I had almost / forgot'. He is established here as an honest figure who gets to the heart of things and is not afraid to speak his mind.

His appreciation of Egypt and its queen, together with his wit and humour, makes him the perfect vehicle for the exotic description of Cleopatra given to his peers from Caesar's entourage. Coming as it does from him, this picture acquires a special authority. Though he is not a subtle politician, he is not without tact when he tries to stop Pompey making remarks to Antony about Julius Caesar's relations with Cleopatra. He then tells Pompey that he does not like him much but is prepared to give him his due. Pompey acknowledges his 'plainness' (II.6.78), his honesty in speaking.

In a witty exchange with Pompey's lieutenant Menas, Enobarbus is loyal to Antony, but frankly says that 'He will to his Egyptian dish again' (II.6.124) and predicts that the marriage to Octavia will prove a cause of friction between Caesar and Antony rather than a bond. He joins in the merrymaking on board Pompey's galley, and mocks the hung-over Lepidus the morning after. Before Antony and Caesar come to blows, he is established as a truthful, honourable, witty and worldly fellow who is clear-sighted in his political and personal judgements.

When it comes to the conflict, he tries unsuccessfully to persuade Cleopatra not to be present personally in Antony's camp and he argues forcefully against the decision to fight by sea. He reports the

CHECK THE FILM
Despite differences in their rank, the relationship between Enobarbus and Antony as fellow soldiers is more than that of master and servant. There is a natural sympathy between them that may be called a product of male bonding. This is very apparent in the 1972 BBC film version.

QUESTION
Enobarbus is equally at home in Rome and Egypt; he is not like the censorious Roman soldiers who open the play, nor does he judge Antony as do Pompey and Caesar. He moves easily between the two poles of the main **antithetical** divide. How, therefore, can his character and role be accounted for by those who see the play turning on the opposition between Roman and Egyptian values?

flight of Cleopatra and after the naval disaster says that he will stay with Antony though it is against reason. His first thoughts of desertion, which he rejects, are prompted by Antony's self-betrayal, partially acknowledged by Antony himself when he says, 'I have fled myself' (III.11.7). When Cleopatra asks him who is to blame, he tells her directly that nobody forced Antony to follow when she fled; he is to blame.

In a series of asides, he comments on the folly of Antony's personal challenge to Caesar, on his own folly on following a fool, and makes sardonic comments on the response of first Cleopatra and then Antony in their dealings and treatment of Caesar's messenger. In a soliloquy – 'Now he'll outstare the lightning' (III.13.194–200) – he sees through Antony's bombastic rhetoric, implying that it is final evidence of the overthrow of all reason, and he comes to his decision to leave Antony. He has clarified the meaning of the action and acts almost as an incarnation of Antony's reasonable self when this has departed from Antony; his departure coincides with Antony's loss of judgement.

After the assertion of reason, emotion comes to the fore in the final phase. As Antony addresses his servants as if for the last time, Enobarbus protests that he is 'onion-eyed' (IV.2.35); Antony is unmanning the troops. Antony's reaction to his desertion, 'O, my fortunes have / Corrupted honest men!' (IV.5.16–7), and his decision to send his treasure to him confirm in the action of the play all that is said of Antony's 'bounty', which is otherwise only hearsay. The guilt felt by Enobarbus and his subsequent depression and loss of will are a counterpoint to the temporary and insecurely founded elation on Antony's side and are a product of the general disintegration that afflicts the affairs of Antony in the war with Caesar. But his death in mental torment and the consciousness of disgrace are proof of the fact that Antony's 'fortunes have / Corrupted honest men' and give a wider dimension to the **tragedy** of the protagonists.

As well as being a reliable guide offering a perspective of common sense in both political and personal matters in a play of many shifts, moods and manoeuvres, his role is to be a kind of shadow attached to the larger figure of Antony. His fate proves to be indissolubly linked

QUESTION
Through the character of Enobarbus are refracted nearly all the various facets that make up the play as a whole, its comedy and tragedy, its imaginative flights, its appreciation of distinctively Roman and distinctively Egyptian attitudes. In the light of this, is it right to limit Enobarbus to the role of chorus to which he has traditionally been assigned?

to his master. And the death of Enobarbus, unheroic but undeluded, is a counterpoint and prelude to what is to come. In the play's construction, his is not merely a supporting role, like those of Charmian and Iras; it is more intricately implicated in the general design; always a clarifying role, what it clarifies at the end is the tragic betrayal of honour in the world that is disintegrating around Antony.

LANGUAGE

The language of Shakespeare's plays, like the theatre for which they were written, contains a wide variety of elements from high to low. The language of *Antony and Cleopatra* shares stylistic features that are common in varying degrees to all Shakespeare's plays. For instance, Samuel Johnson memorably remarked on Shakespeare's fondness for wordplay: 'A quibble was to him the fatal Cleopatra for which he lost the world and was content to lose it' (quoted in *Johnson on Shakespeare*, edited by Walter Raleigh, OUP, 1908, p. 24). This talent for wordplay may unexpectedly transform the commonplace, as when the argumentative Cleopatra impudently asks Antony, 'Can Fulvia die?' (I.3.58). This single pun, playing on the secondary meaning of the word 'die' which refers in Elizabethan English to the sexual climax, might be said to represent in miniature the **tragicomic** vision of life embodied in so many of the plays. Wordplay in Shakespeare, like death, is a great leveller; even the straight-laced Caesar is not above a pun as he royally complains that in Antony's absence 'we do bear / So great weight in his lightness' (I.4.24–5), lightness referring both to neglect of duty and levity.

There is, however, something distinctive about the language of this play to which reference has already been made in the **Detailed summaries**. Its grand vision of things is created and sustained by its grand language. The use of **hyperbole**, the **figure of speech** which emphasises through exaggeration, is particularly pronounced in speeches made by Antony and Cleopatra and in speeches made about them. Hyperbole is apparent in the very first speech of the play. In describing Antony's 'dotage' that 'O'erflows the measure' (I.1.1–2), Philo says Antony's heart, which formerly in fights 'hath burst / The buckles on his breast' (a somewhat heightened version of the truth), now 'is become the bellows and the fan / To cool a

 CHECK THE NET

For various sources relating to Shakespeare's grammar, syntax and vocabulary, and for the differences between Shakespearean and modern English, see http://www.bardweb.net

 CHECK THE BOOK

For an general introduction, see 'The Language of Shakespeare' by David Crystal in *Shakespeare: An Oxford Guide*, edited by Stanley Wells and Lena Cowen Orlin (OUP, 2003); for an essay on the language of this play, see the chapter in Frank Kermode, *Shakespeare's Language* (Penguin, 2000); for Shakespearean punning, see M. M. Mahood, *Shakespeare's Wordplay* (Methuen, 1957).

gypsy's lust', where the action of the heart is again represented by an exaggerated figure of speech (I.1.7–10). Earlier 'his goodly eyes' were said to have 'glowed like plated Mars' (I.1.2–4), that is, like the war god in shining armour, where the grand simile has a heightening effect.

In an equally grand comparison, Cleopatra is likened to Venus. There are many mythological references which serve to put the characters in an exalted light which supports their own sense of their high status; Cleopatra is reported to have appeared 'In th'habiliments of the goddess Isis' (III.6.17), the Egyptian goddess of the moon. References to the moon, the sun and the stars give a cosmic dimension to this hyperbolic style: 'Alack, our terrene moon / Is now eclipsed, and it portends alone / The fall of Antony' (III.13.153–5). The grand note is further sustained in allusions to the elements, as in Cleopatra's declaration that 'I am fire and air; my other elements / I give to baser life' (V.2.288–9), and in the following hyperboles: 'I, that with my sword / Quartered the world, and o'er green Neptune's back / With ships made cities' (IV.14.57–9) and 'His legs bestrid the ocean' (V.2.82). All this is probably what led Samuel Taylor Coleridge (1772–1834), in a much repeated phrase, to speak of the 'happy valiancy' of the style in this play, its felicitous daring.

In addition to the use of hyperbole and the grand comparison, which may be regarded as a complement to hyperbole, the language of the play is marked by the use of various figures of wit (the poetic intelligence), like **paradox** (an unexpected, apparently illogical or self-contradictory statement), **oxymoron** (the union of opposites) and **conceit** (a far-fetched comparison). Many of these figures are associated with Cleopatra and used to express her 'infinite variety' (II.2.241 – see **Extended commentaries**). These figures of wit are often employed for comic purposes; for example, Enobarbus, on hearing of the death of Fulvia, likens the gods to the tailors of the earth in removing worn-out robes and extends the conceit over several lines (I.2.162–71). But they are also to be found at moments of high seriousness, as when Antony declares to Eros, 'with a wound I must be cured' (IV.14.78), and after Eros has killed himself and Antony is about to fall on his sword, Antony plays on the idea of teaching and learning, invoking Eros with the words, 'Thy master dies thy scholar' (IV.14.102).

CHECK THE BOOK

Much can be gained from Richard Lanham, *A Handbook of Rhetorical Terms: A Guide for Students of English Literature* (University of California Press, 1969), and from Sister Miriam Joseph, *Rhetoric in Shakespeare's Time* (Harcourt, 1962).

There are also recurrent patterns of imagery, some of which can be mentioned briefly here with one or two prominent examples. Food and drink are particularly, though not exclusively, associated with Egypt: 'Now no more / The juice of Egypt's grape shall moist this lip' (V.2.280–1). Egypt is a place of pleasure, but also of mystery and danger, encapsulated in the Nile imagery particularly involving the serpent. Cleopatra herself reports Antony addressing her as his 'serpent of old Nile' (I.5.25). Antony's sword is a material object, but it is also a recurring symbol of his military prowess and masculine identity. In a play in which the main characters are intensely conscious of their public status and of their grand self-images – 'But since my lord / Is Antony again, I will be Cleopatra' (III.13.185–6) – there are allusions to acting and the theatre. Cleopatra tauntingly bids Antony, 'play one scene / Of excellent dissembling' (I.3.78–9), and in her mind's eye sees 'Some squeaking Cleopatra boy my greatness' (V.2.220). There is great irony and wit in this, given that the part of Cleopatra on the Jacobean stage, like all women's parts, would have been played by a boy.

CHECK THE BOOK

See sections on the play in Caroline F. E. Spurgeon, *Shakespeare's Imagery and What It Tells Us* (CUP, 1935), and Wolfgang Clemen, *The Development of Shakespeare's Imagery* (Methuen, 1951).

Finally there is a complex of ideas associated with the word 'fortune', which can mean luck, success or perhaps fate, depending on the context. At the root of its use is the medieval image of the goddess Fortuna, the turning of whose wheel changes irreversibly the fortunes of her mortal underlings. The interpreter of fortune in Egypt is cryptic in his responses to Cleopatra's maids. In a pivotal scene, Antony asks the soothsayer whose fortunes shall rise higher, his or Caesar's. As a result of the reply he leaves Rome. After the first battle, 'Fortune and Antony part here' (IV.12.19). Caesar is 'full-fortuned' (IV.15.24), though, as far as Cleopatra is concerned, 'Not being Fortune, he's but Fortune's knave' (V.2.3), and with Antony she mocks 'The luck of Caesar' (V.2.285). In the general design this chain of imagery serves to give **unity** to the plot; it also has the effect of hinting at an inevitable destiny underlying the surface of the play's action and working through the decisions and errors of the human participants.

PART FOUR

CRITICAL HISTORY

EARLY RESPONSES

There is no evidence that *Antony and Cleopatra* was revived in the seventeenth century after its first performance; indeed, in the absence of any precise record some scholars have doubted whether it was actually performed in Shakespeare's lifetime. Nor is there much evidence that, unlike other plays of Shakespeare such as *Hamlet*, it was part of the common stock of the educated person's reading and repertoire. Dryden had written his version of the story of Antony and Cleopatra in 1677, the simplicity of which is reflected in his title *All for Love, or The World Well Lost* (this gives Shakespeare's more ambiguous play a definite 'romantic' slant). From this point the history of the two plays was intertwined for the next one hundred and fifty years. Dryden's play, which obeyed the **unities** of time, place and action, was more in accord with the dramatic theory and practice of what is sometimes called the **neoclassical** period extending from the second half of seventeenth century to the end of the eighteenth. In this period it was revived several times.

 **CHECK
THE BOOK**
The history of early
and subsequent
productions is fully
described with
illustrations in The
New Cambridge
Shakespeare, edited
by David Bevington
(1990): see '*Antony
and Cleopatra* in
performance',
pp. 44–70.

The first revival of Shakespeare's play came in 1759 and was mounted by the famous actor manager David Garrick. However, it was not reproduced intact and there were many scenic rearrangements with Shakespeare's forty-two scenes being reduced to twenty-seven. Changes in location were restricted; some characters and many of the bawdy lines were excised. The political element was played down to give the love affair greater prominence. It was not a success.

Dryden continued to be revived well into the nineteenth century. In 1813 there was a production that amalgamated features from both Dryden and Shakespeare. It was not until 1849 that Samuel Phelps successfully mounted a sumptuous production of Shakespeare's play, though not without considerable cutting and scenic rearrangement, which finally supplanted Dryden's. The realistic style of nineteenth-century production, in which costumes and sets were researched with an archaeological precision, was very different from the spare style of the Elizabethan theatre where there was little scenery and where costumes were contemporary. This made it virtually impossible to reproduce Shakespeare's text with its great variety of scenes changes without quite major adjustment. It was not until this style was abandoned in the 1920s that the Shakespeare text that we know was deemed suitable for continuous performance. There is a vindication of the play's construction for stage performance by Harley Granville-Barker in his *Prefaces to Shakespeare* (1930).

Despite the lateness of its revival in the theatre, there is evidence to suggest that after the neoclassical period had ended (when the play's irregularity in breaking the unities and mixing the genres was a stumbling block to its appreciation), the play was highly thought of in the nineteenth century. William Hazlitt in *Characters of Shakespear's Plays* (1817) wrote lyrically of the character of Cleopatra. The Romantic poet Coleridge praised its poetry and asked whether it might rank alongside the four great **tragedies** which had immediately preceded it, *Hamlet* (1600–1), *Othello* (1602–4), *King Lear* (1605–6) and *Macbeth* (1605–6). This question has been taken up by A. C. Bradley in 'Shakespeare's *Antony and Cleopatra*', published in *Oxford Lectures on Poetry* (1909). Remarking on the sparse dramatic action, the lack of an inner struggle evident in Antony as he leaves first Cleopatra and then Octavia, the spirit of irony that pervades the political aspects of the play, a lack of awareness in Cleopatra that she has destroyed Antony, and the theatrical self-awareness of the protagonists, particularly Cleopatra, Bradley gives the answer no; for all its magnificence the play does not engage its audience as the earlier tragedies do.

The traditional tendency of earlier criticism to emphasise the transcendent vision of ennobling love, perhaps reaching its height in G. Wilson Knight's *The Imperial Theme* (OUP, 1931), has led to a reaction that is more sceptical; on the one hand there are those like H. A. Mason in *Shakespeare's Tragedies of Love* (Chatto and Windus, 1970), who see a weakness in the dramatic exploration of the play's theme which is not compensated for by the poetry; on the other, those who find its uncertainties and ambiguities deliberate,

CHECK THE BOOK

These texts can be found in the revised edition of the casebook on *Antony and Cleopatra* edited by John Russell Brown (Macmillan, 1991).

CHECK THE NET

The full text of A.C. Bradley's famous *Shakespearean Tragedy* is available at http://www. clicknotes.com/ bradley stressing the double view the play offers of its protagonists in love and politics, such as Janet Adelman in *The Common Liar: An Essay on Antony and Cleopatra* (Yale University Press, 1973).

RECENT READINGS

CHECK THE BOOK
There is a survey of recent theory criticism relating to the play in Drakakis's extensive introduction to *Antony and Cleopatra* (New Casebooks, Macmillan, 1994).

As a play that deals with central issues of sexuality and power, *Antony and Cleopatra* continues to generate new analyses prompted by the new ways of looking at texts and analysing them that have become common in literary studies in recent years. In general it may be said that there has been a greater emphasis on political aspects of the play and in the wake of feminist criticism much interest in the issues of gender raised by the representation of the masculine and feminine in the play.

The tendency to regard Shakespeare's plays as transcending their time – perhaps most marked in the case of the Roman plays, which do not have any immediately perceived connection with the British scene – has been subject to a variety of challenges in recent accounts. In *Radical Tragedy: Religion, Ideology and Power in the Drama of Shakespeare and His Contemporaries* (Harvester Press, 1984) Jonathan Dollimore argues that the plays represent on the stage a radical questioning of the traditional forms of authority in Church and state; this questioning or interrogation may be related to the later collapse of these traditional forms resulting in the Civil War that began in the reign of Charles I. In the case of *Antony and Cleopatra*, Dollimore argues that the conflict between Antony and Caesar represents a collision between older conceptions of power centred upon individual honour (associated with the old aristocracy) and a new conception of civil power in which personal honour is no longer the dominant factor. Antony is caught between the two. His relationship with Cleopatra is a kind of power play, reflecting the larger play of political power. Antony's love turns out to be a compensation for the loss of power. Far from being transcendent, the love affair is determined by relations of power.

A more specific account of the play's relation to history is to be found in 'Jacobean *Antony and Cleopatra*' (1985) where

H. Neville Davies (in *Antony and Cleopatra*, New Casebooks,
edited by John Drakakis) argues that the play had an immediate
historical parallel in Jacobean court politics with James I
representing himself as the British Augustus (Octavius Caesar took
the name Augustus after his return from the east) maintaining peace
in a united kingdom. The action of the play records the movement
from triumvirate to universal monarchy; Caesar prophesies that
'The time of universal peace is near' (IV.6.5). On this reading, since
the play shows Caesar in an unflattering light, it can be regarded as
sceptical and unsupportive of these claims of Jacobean propaganda.
Related to this is the section on the play by Leonard Tennenhouse
in *Power on Display: The Politics of Shakespeare's Genres* (Methuen,
1986, included in *Shakespeare: The Roman Plays*, edited by Graham
Holderness et al.). He examines the process of representing
Cleopatra in the light of the ways in which the various images of
Elizabeth I were constructed, and endeavours to show that
Shakespeare provides a post-Elizabethan image of female monarchy.

CHECK THE BOOK

The volume of essays collected by Graham Holderness, Bryan Loughrey and Andrew Murphy (Longman, 1996) is particularly concerned to relate the Roman plays to their English historical context.

In the general debate about issues of gender that has been stimulated
by the feminist movement, particular interest has focused on
whether there is an essential difference between male and female
(other than obvious biological difference) or whether gender roles
are socially constructed. This has stimulated greater awareness of
the representation of masculine and feminine in the play. Traditional
'Roman' ideas of masculinity represented by Caesar (see especially
his speech denouncing Antony for subverting the traditional
masculine role at I.4.1–10 and the confirmation of this in what
Cleopatra says at II.5.22–3) may be seen to be threatened by
Egyptian feminisation; alternatively Antony may represent a new
more androgynous masculinity. This is substantially the starting
point of Janet Adelman in 'Making Defect Perfection' from
*Suffocating Mothers: Fantasies of Maternal Origin in Shakespeare's
Plays* (Routledge, 1992). She sees Cleopatra 'as facilitating the
evocation of a new image of Antony's masculinity – an image
predicated on her own imaginative fecundity' (reproduced in
Shakespeare: The Roman Plays, edited by Graham Holderness et al.,
p. 71). Another feminist study that focuses more on Antony than
Cleopatra is that of Coppélia Kahn in *Roman Shakespeare:
Warriors, Wounds, and Women* (Routledge, 1997).

QUESTION
Can Cleopatra be both a feminist icon and a projection of masculine fantasy?

CONTEXT
Mediterranean Romans would probably not have attached much significance to the skin colour of a woman descended from Ptolemy (one of the generals of Alexander the Great who inherited the Egyptian part of his empire), who was actually of Greek origin. Differences with Cleopatra and Egypt for the Romans were more than skin deep; they rested on questions of politics and economics (the corn supply) rather than culture or race.

Equally there is a debate about the extent to which Cleopatra might simply be an exotic version of the old stereotypes or whether she represents a powerful and positive new image for women (and men). In a polemical essay, 'Egyptian Queens and Male Reviewers: Sexist Attitudes in *Antony and Cleopatra* Criticism' (1977), Linda T. Fitz (in *Antony and Cleopatra*, New Casebooks, edited by John Drakakis) takes issue with what she sees as the alternative views of traditional (man-made and male-oriented) criticism: either Antony is destroyed in his 'dotage' by a treacherous strumpet, or the play celebrates a transcendent love, both views precluding a reasonable assessment of Cleopatra. She argues that many male critics feel personally threatened by the powerful Egyptian, revealing deep fears of aggressive or manipulative women. Equally, the fascination with her mysterious inscrutability can be seen as masking the common male view that all women are unfathomable (and probably irrational and whimsical). She argues that Cleopatra needs to be demystified and that her variety is finite. She laments the unwillingness of male critics to consider Cleopatra as a **tragic** protagonist on a level with Antony.

In the light of the radical feminist critique of western culture by Luce Irigaray, Mary Hamer in 'Reading *Antony and Cleopatra* Through Irigaray's *Speculum*' (in *Antony and Cleopatra*, edited by Nigel Wood, Open University Press, 1996) argues that when Shakespeare came to give a voice to Cleopatra, he discovered how she destabilised 'the old story about women and desire' (p. 74). He gives her a voice that offers an alternative way of seeing things, that differs from the Roman view: 'Finding this voice becomes the project of the play: that is why it will continue for a whole act after the death of Antony' (p. 75). Hamer stresses the community of feeling in the final act between the women. Kahn, by contrast, argues that with the 'identification of the marble constancy of death with marital consummation: "Husband, I come!"' (p. 139), much of the power of Cleopatra at the end 'derives from its honorific identity of wife that this mode of death grants her'.

The character of Cleopatra raises questions not only about the representation of women but, since she is conceived as 'tawny fronted', of black women too. Though Plutarch makes little of her racial difference, as in Shakespeare, Cleopatra is a representative of a culture that has values not usually associated with the Romans.

The cultural difference is there in Shakespeare, though it is not as accentuated as it could have been or as some commentators maintain. Cleopatra appears 'In th'habiliments of the goddess Isis' (III.6.17) when she is formally endowed with kingdoms by Antony (here the affront is political; from Caesar's point of view Antony had no business creating a power centre to rival Rome). She nevertheless speaks in the language of the Graeco-Roman tradition; her gods and heroes – Hercules, Mars, Juno, Mercury and Jove – are those of Greece and Rome.

In the wake of Edward W. Said's *Orientalism: Western Concepts of the Orient* (Routledge & Kegan Paul, 1978), the representation of Cleopatra, alluring, magnificent, enchanting and exotic, has been seen as a typical western mystification of the oriental; a figment of the imagination that fails to be credible when viewed from a non-western perspective. In post-imperial times, too, Cleopatra in her relations with the Romans is seen to be fighting Roman imperialism. In 'Representing Cleopatra in the Post-colonial Moment' Dympna Callaghan (in *Antony and Cleopatra*, edited by Nigel Wood) asks a question prompted by the theoretical analysis of Gayatri Spivak in her essay 'Can the Subaltern Speak?' Can Cleopatra speak for those who have been oppressed, marginalised and silenced in western patriarchal society? Callaghan asks: 'Can Cleopatra function as anything other than an exotic, racially marked heroine who is yet another manifestation of "orientalism"?' She analyses Cleopatra as a representation 'which tells us not about femininity, Egyptian or otherwise, but about the Western masculinity which fantasized her into existence' (p. 53). Her answer seems to be no.

> **CONTEXT**
>
> In history, after her suicide, Caesar annexed Egypt for the empire and it became a Roman province.

PART FIVE

BACKGROUND

WILLIAM SHAKESPEARE'S LIFE

There are no personal records of Shakespeare's life. Official documents and occasional references to him by contemporary dramatists enable us to draw the main outline of his public life, but his private life remains hidden. Although not at all unusual for a writer of his time, this lack of first-hand evidence has tempted many to read his plays as personal records and to look in them for clues to his character and convictions. The results are unconvincing, partly because Renaissance art was not subjective or designed primarily to express its creator's personality, and partly because the drama of any period is very difficult to read biographically. Except when plays are written by committed dramatists to promote social or political causes (as by Shaw or Brecht), it is all but impossible to decide who among the variety of fictional characters in a drama represents the dramatist, or which of the various and often conflicting points of view expressed is authorial.

 CHECK THE BOOK
There are a number of biographies of Shakespeare – many of them very speculative – but the most authoritative is still Samuel Schoenbaum's *Shakespeare: A Documentary Life* (OUP, 1975).

What we do know can be quickly summarised. Shakespeare was born into a well-to-do family in the market town of Stratford-upon-Avon in Warwickshire, where he was baptised, in Holy Trinity Church, on 26 April 1564. His father, John Shakespeare, was a prosperous glover and leather merchant who became a person of some importance in the town: in 1565 he was elected an alderman of the town, and in 1568 he became high bailiff (or mayor) of Stratford. In 1557 he had married Mary Arden. Their third child (of eight) and eldest son, William, learnt to read and write at the primary (or 'petty') school in Stratford and then, it seems probable, attended the local grammar school, where he would have studied Latin, history, logic and rhetoric. In November 1582 William, then aged eighteen, married Anne Hathaway, who was twenty-six years old. They had a daughter, Susanna, in May 1583, and twins, Hamnet and Judith, in 1585.

Shakespeare next appears in the historical record in 1592 when he was mentioned as a London actor and playwright in a pamphlet by the dramatist Robert Greene. These 'lost years' 1585–92 have been the subject of much speculation, but how they were occupied remains as much a mystery as when Shakespeare left Stratford, and why. In his pamphlet, *Greene's Groatsworth of Wit*, Greene expresses to his fellow dramatists his outrage that the 'upstart crow' Shakespeare has the impudence to believe he 'is as well able to bombast out a blank verse as the best of you'. To have aroused this hostility from a rival, Shakespeare must, by 1592, have been long enough in London to have made a name for himself as a playwright. We may conjecture that he had left Stratford in 1586 or 1587.

During the next twenty years, Shakespeare continued to live in London, regularly visiting his wife and family in Stratford. He continued to act, but his chief fame was as a dramatist. From 1594 he wrote exclusively for the Lord Chamberlain's Men, which rapidly became the leading dramatic company and from 1603 enjoyed the patronage of James I as the King's Men. His plays were extremely popular and he became a shareholder in his theatre company. He was able to buy lands around Stratford and a large house in the town, to which he retired about 1611. He died there on 23 April 1616 and was buried in Holy Trinity Church on 25 April.

www. CHECK THE NET
You can read Shakespeare's will in his own handwriting – and in modern transcription – online at the Public Records Office: http://www.pro.gov.uk/virtualmuseum and search for 'Shakespeare'.

SHAKESPEARE'S DRAMATIC CAREER

Between the late 1580s and 1613 Shakespeare wrote thirty-seven plays, and contributed to some by other dramatists. This was by no means an exceptional number for a professional playwright of the times. The exact date of the composition of individual plays is a matter of debate – for only a few plays is the date of their first performance known – but the broad outlines of Shakespeare's dramatic career have been established. He began in the late 1580s and early 1590s by rewriting earlier plays and working with plotlines inspired by the classics. He concentrated on comedies (such as *The Comedy of Errors*, 1590–4, which derived from the Latin playwright Plautus) and plays dealing with English history (such as the three parts of *Henry VI*, 1589–92), though he also tried his hand at bloodthirsty revenge tragedy (*Titus Andronicus*, 1592–3, indebted to both Ovid and Seneca). During the 1590s Shakespeare developed his expertise in these kinds of play to write comic masterpieces such as *A Midsummer Night's Dream* (1594–5) and *As You Like It* (1599–1600) and history plays such as *Henry IV* (1596–8) and *Henry V* (1598–9). The two parts of *Henry IV*, in which Falstaff, one of his most

SHAKESPEARE'S DRAMATIC CAREER continued

CHECK THE FILM
There are lots of anachronisms and inaccuracies in *Shakespeare in Love* (1998) – that's half the fun of it – but its depiction of the hand-to-mouth world of the commercial theatre has something of the energy and edginess from which Shakespeare drew his artistic power.

popular comic characters, appears, have a mixture of comic and serious scenes and public and private worlds like *Antony and Cleopatra*. The fascination he shows for the related subjects of politics and the exercise of power is manifest in his first major Roman play, *Julius Caesar* (1598–1600). It is one of the advantages of the Roman setting that, in an age when plays were censored, this fascination can be pursued with a freedom and a detachment not possible in representing contemporary events or recent history.

As the new century begins a new note is detectable. Plays such a *Troilus and Cressida* (1601–2) and *Measure for Measure* (1603–4), poised between comedy and **tragedy**, evoke complex responses. Because of their generic uncertainty and ambivalent tone such works are sometimes referred to as 'problem plays'. *Antony and Cleopatra* has occasionally been set alongside these for comparison, though it is more usually discussed, together with *Coriolanus*, the third great Roman play (1605–10), in comparison with the four great tragedies which it immediately follows: *Hamlet* (1600–1), *Othello* (1602–4), *King Lear* (1605–6) and *Macbeth* (1605–6). These six plays constitute Shakespeare's tragic period. *Antony and Cleopatra*, as a tragedy of love, may be fruitfully juxtaposed with *Othello*. These two plays and *Coriolanus* all feature great military heroes who come to grief through an inability to manage the personal and emotional side of their lives.

In the last years of his dramatic career, Shakespeare wrote a group of plays of a quite different kind. These 'romances', as they are often called, are in many ways the most remarkable of all his plays. The group comprises *Pericles* (1608), *Cymbeline* (1609–11), *The Winter's Tale* (1610–11) and *The Tempest* (1610–11). These plays (particularly *Cymbeline*) reprise many of the situations and themes of the earlier dramas but in fantastical and exotic dramatic designs which, set in distant lands, covering large tracts of time and involving music, mime, dance and tableaux, have something of the qualities of masques and pageants. The situations which in the tragedies had led to disaster are here resolved: the great theme is restoration and reconciliation. Where in the tragedies Ophelia, Desdemona and Cordelia died, the daughters of these plays – Marina, Imogen, Perdita, Miranda – survive and are reunited with their parents and lovers.

THE TEXTS OF SHAKESPEARE'S PLAYS

Nineteen of Shakespeare's plays were printed during his lifetime in what are called 'quartos' (books, each containing one play, and made up of sheets of paper each folded twice to make four leaves). Shakespeare, however, did not supervise their publication. This was not unusual. When a playwright had sold a play to a dramatic company he sold his rights in it: copyright belonged to whoever had possession of an actual copy of the text, and so consequently authors had no control over what happened to their work. Anyone who could get hold of the text of a play might publish it if they wished. Hence, what found its way into print might be the author's copy, but it might be an actor's copy or prompt copy, perhaps cut or altered for performance; sometimes, actors (or even members of the audience) might publish what they could remember of the text. Printers, working without the benefit of the author's oversight, introduced their own errors, through misreading the manuscript, for example, and by 'correcting' what seemed to them not to make sense.

In 1623 John Heminges and Henry Condell, two actors in Shakespeare's company, collected together texts of thirty-six of Shakespeare's plays (*Pericles* was omitted) and published them in a large folio (a book in which each sheet of paper is folded once in half, to give two leaves). This, the First Folio, was followed by later editions in 1632, 1663 and 1685. Despite its appearance of authority, however, the texts in the First Folio still present many difficulties, for there are printing errors and confused passages in the plays, and its texts often differ significantly from those of the earlier quartos, when these exist.

Shakespeare's texts have, then, been through a number of intermediaries. We do not have his authority for any one of his plays, and hence we cannot know exactly what it was that he wrote. Bibliographers, textual critics and editors have spent a great deal of effort on endeavouring to get behind the errors, uncertainties and contradictions in the available texts to recover the plays as Shakespeare originally wrote them. What we read is the result of these efforts. Modern texts are what editors have constructed from the available evidence: they correspond to no sixteenth- or seventeenth-century editions, and to no early performance of a

> **CONTEXT**
>
> A quarto is a small format book, roughly equivalent to a modern paperback. Play texts in quarto form typically cost sixpence, as opposed to the cost of going to the theatre at a penny.

> **CONTEXT**
>
> Plays were not considered as serious literature in this period: when, in 1612, Sir Thomas Bodley was setting up his library in Oxford, he instructed his staff not to buy any drama for the collection: 'haply [perhaps] some plays may be worthy the keeping, but hardly one in forty'.

CHECK THE NET
You can find out more about the earliest editions of Shakespeare at the University of Pennsylvania's ERIC site: http://oldsite.library. upenn.edu/etext/ collections/furness/ eric/eric.html

Shakespeare play. Furthermore, these composite texts differ from each other, for different editors read the early texts differently and come to different conclusions. A Shakespeare text is an unstable and a contrived thing.

Often, of course, its judgements embody, if not the personal prejudices of the editor, then the cultural preferences of the time in which he or she was working. Growing awareness of this has led recent scholars to distrust the whole editorial enterprise and to repudiate the attempt to construct a 'perfect' text. Stanley Wells and Gary Taylor, the editors of the Oxford edition of *The Complete Works* (1988), point out that almost certainly the texts of Shakespeare's plays were altered in performance, and from one performance to another, so that there may never have been a single version. They note, too, that Shakespeare probably revised and rewrote some plays. They do not claim to print a definitive text of any play, but prefer what seems to them the 'more theatrical' version, and when there is a great difference between available versions, as with *King Lear*, they print two texts.

SHAKESPEARE AND THE ENGLISH RENAISSANCE

Shakespeare arrived in London at the very time that the Elizabethan period was poised to become the 'golden age' of English literature. Although Elizabeth reigned as queen from 1558 to 1603, the term 'Elizabethan' is used very loosely in a literary sense to refer to the period 1580 to 1625, when the great works of the age were produced. (Sometimes the later part of this period is distinguished as 'Jacobean', from the Latin form of the name of the king who succeeded Elizabeth, James I of England and VI of Scotland, who reigned from 1603 to 1625.) The poet Edmund Spenser (1552–99) heralded this new age with his pastoral poem *The Shepheardes Calender* (1579), *A Defence of Poesy* and in his essay (written about 1580, although not published until 1595) his friend Sir Philip Sidney (1554–86) championed the imaginative power of the 'speaking picture of poesy', famously declaring that 'Nature never set forth the earth in so rich tapestry as diverse poets have done . . . her world is brazen, the poets only deliver a golden.'

Spenser and Sidney were part of that rejuvenating movement in European culture which since the nineteenth century has been known by the term 'Renaissance'. Meaning literally 'rebirth' it denotes a revival and redirection of artistic and intellectual endeavour which began in Italy in the fourteenth century in the poetry of Petrarch (1304–74). It spread gradually northwards across Europe, and is first detectable in England in the early sixteenth century in the writings of the scholar and statesman Sir Thomas More (1478–1535) and in the poetry of Sir Thomas Wyatt (1503–42) and Henry Howard, Earl of Surrey (*c*.1517–47). Its keynote was a curiosity in thought which challenged old assumptions and traditions. To the innovative spirit of the Renaissance, the preceding ages appeared dully unoriginal and conformist.

That spirit was fuelled by the rediscovery of many classical texts and the culture of Greece and Rome. This fostered a confidence in human reason and in human potential which, in every sphere, challenged old convictions. The discovery of America and its peoples (Christopher Columbus had sailed in 1492) demonstrated that the world was a larger and stranger place than had been thought. The cosmological speculation of Copernicus (later confirmed by Galileo) that the sun, not the earth, was the centre of our planetary system challenged the centuries-old belief that the earth and human beings were at the centre of the cosmos. The pragmatic political philosophy of Machiavelli (1469–1527) seemed to cut politics free from its traditional link with morality by permitting to statesmen any means which secured the desired end. And the religious movements we know collectively as the Reformation broke with the Church of Rome and set the individual conscience, not ecclesiastical authority, at the centre of the religious life. Nothing, it seemed, was beyond questioning, nothing impossible.

Shakespeare's drama is innovative and challenging in exactly the way of the Renaissance. It questions the beliefs, assumptions and politics upon which Elizabethan society was founded. And although the plays always conclude in a restoration of order and stability, many critics are inclined to argue that their imaginative energy goes into subverting, rather than reinforcing, traditional values. Convention, audience expectation and censorship all required the status quo to be endorsed by the plots' conclusions,

CHECK THE NET
You can consult texts by Spenser and Sidney, and other contemporaries of Shakespeare, at Renascence Editions http://www. uoregon.edu/ ~rbear/ren.htm

CHECK THE NET
The Luminarium site has links to a wide range of historical information on sixteenth-century topics including astronomy, medicine, economics and technology: http://www. luminarium.org

but the dramas find ways to allow alternative sentiments to be expressed. Frequently, figures of authority are undercut by some comic or parodic figure. Despairing, critical, dissident, disillusioned, unbalanced, rebellious, mocking voices are repeatedly to be heard in the plays, rejecting, resenting, defying the established order. They belong always to marginal, socially unacceptable figures, 'licensed', as it were, by their situations to say what would be unacceptable from socially privileged or responsible citizens. The question is: are such characters given these views to discredit them, or were they the only ones through whom a voice could be given to radical and dissident ideas? Is Shakespeare a conservative or a revolutionary?

CHECK THE BOOK

Benedict Anderson's book on the rise of the nation and nationalism, *Imagined Communities* (Verso Books, revised edition, 1991), has been influential for its definition of the nation as 'an imagined political community' – imagined in part through cultural productions such as Shakespeare's history plays.

Renaissance culture was intensely nationalistic. With the break-up of the internationalism of the Middle Ages the evolving nation states which still mark the map of Europe began for the first time to acquire distinctive cultural identities. There was intense rivalry among them as they sought to achieve in their own vernacular languages a culture which could equal that of Greece and Rome. Spenser's great allegorical epic poem *The Faerie Queene*, which began to appear from 1590, celebrated Elizabeth and was intended to outdo the poetic achievements of France and Italy and to stand beside works of Virgil and Homer. Shakespeare is equally preoccupied with national identity. His history plays tell an epic story which examines how modern England came into being through the conflicts of the fifteenth-century Wars of the Roses which brought the Tudors to the throne. He is fascinated, too, by the related subject of politics and the exercise of power. With the collapse of medieval feudalism and the authority of local barons, the royal court in the Renaissance came to assume a new status as the centre of power and patronage. It was here that the destiny of a country was shaped. Courts, and how to succeed in them, consequently fascinated the Renaissance; and they fascinated Shakespeare and his audience.

But the dramatic gaze is not merely admiring; through a variety of devices, a critical perspective is brought to bear. The court may be paralleled by a very different world, revealing uncomfortable similarities (for example, Henry's court and the Boar's Head tavern, ruled over by Falstaff in *Henry IV*). Its hypocrisy may be bitterly denounced (for example, in the diatribes of the mad Lear) and its self-seeking ambition represented disturbingly in the figure of a

Machiavellian villain (such as Edmund in *King Lear*) or a malcontent (such as Iago in *Othello*). Shakespeare is fond of displacing the court to another context, the better to examine its assumptions and pretensions and to offer alternatives to the courtly life (for example, in the pastoral setting of the forest of Arden in *As You Like It* or Prospero's island in *The Tempest*). Courtiers are frequently figures of fun whose unmanly sophistication ('neat and trimly dressed, / Fresh as a bridegroom ... perfumed like a milliner', says Hotspur of such a man in *1 Henry IV*, I.3.33–6) is contrasted with plain-speaking integrity: Oswald is set against Kent in *King Lear*.

When thinking of these matters, we should remember that stage plays were subject to censorship, and any criticism had therefore to be muted or oblique: direct criticism of the monarch or contemporary English court would not be tolerated. This has something to do with why Shakespeare's plays are always set either in the past, or abroad.

The nationalism of the English Renaissance was reinforced by Protestantism. Henry VIII had broken with Rome in the 1530s and in Shakespeare's time there was an independent Protestant state Church. Because the Pope in Rome had excommunicated Queen Elizabeth as a heretic and relieved the English of their allegiance to the crown, there was deep suspicion of Roman Catholics as potential traitors. This was enforced by the attempted invasion of the Spanish Armada in 1588. This was a religiously inspired crusade to overthrow Elizabeth and restore England to Roman Catholic allegiance. Roman Catholicism was hence easily identified with hostility to England. Its association with disloyalty and treachery was enforced by the Gunpowder Plot of 1605, a Roman Catholic attempt to destroy the government of England.

Shakespeare's plays are remarkably free from direct religious sentiment, but their emphases are Protestant. Young women, for example, are destined for marriage, not for nunneries (precisely what Isabella appears to escape at the end of *Measure for Measure*); friars are dubious characters, full of schemes and deceptions, if with benign intentions, as in *Much Ado About Nothing* or *Romeo and Juliet*. (We should add, though, that Puritans, extreme Protestants, are even less kindly treated: for example, Malvolio in *Twelfth Night*.)

CHECK THE FILM
We can get a modern equivalent of the effect of this displacement from Christine Edzard's film of *As You Like It* (1992). Here, the court scenes are set in the luxurious headquarters of a bank or company; the woodland scenes amid a sort of 'cardboard city' of social outcasts and the vulnerable.

The central figures of the plays are frequently individuals beset by temptation, by the lure of evil – Angelo in *Measure for Measure*, Othello, Lear, Macbeth – and not only in tragedies: Falstaff is described as 'that old white-bearded Satan' (*1 Henry IV*, II.4.454). We follow their inner struggles. Shakespeare's heroes have the preoccupation with self and the introspective tendencies encouraged by Protestantism: his tragic heroes are haunted by their consciences, seeking their true selves, agonising over what course of action to take as they follow what can often be understood as a kind of spiritual progress towards heaven or hell.

SHAKESPEARE'S THEATRE

CHECK THE NET
Find out more about the Shakespearean theatre at http://www.reading.ac.uk/globe. This web site describes the historical researches undertaken in connection with the Globe Theatre on London's Bankside, which was rebuilt in the late 1990s.

The theatre for which the plays were written was one of the most remarkable innovations of the Renaissance. There had been no theatres or acting companies during the medieval period. Performed on carts and in open spaces at Christian festivals, plays had been almost exclusively religious. Such professional actors as there were wandered the country putting on a variety of entertainments in the yards of inns, on makeshift stages in market squares, or anywhere else suitable. They did not perform full-length plays, but mimes, juggling and comedy acts. Such actors were regarded by officialdom and polite society as little better than vagabonds and layabouts.

Just before Shakespeare went to London all this began to change. A number of young men who had been to the universities of Oxford and Cambridge came to London in the 1580s and began to write plays which made use of what they had learnt about the classical drama of ancient Greece and Rome. Plays such as John Lyly's *Alexander and Campaspe* (1584), Christopher Marlowe's *Tamburlaine the Great* (c.1587) and Thomas Kyd's *The Spanish Tragedy* (1588–9) were unlike anything that had been written in English before. They were full-length plays on secular subjects, taking their plots from history and legend, adopting many of the devices of classical drama, and offering a range of characterisation and situation hitherto unattempted in English drama. With the exception of Lyly's prose dramas, they were in the unrhymed iambic pentameters (blank verse) which the Earl of Surrey had introduced into English earlier in the sixteenth century. This was a freer and more expressive medium than the rhymed verse of medieval drama. It was the drama of these 'university wits' which Shakespeare challenged when he came to London. Greene was one of them, and we have heard how little he liked this Shakespeare setting himself up as a dramatist.

The most significant change of all, however, was that these dramatists wrote for the professional theatre. In 1576 James Burbage built the first permanent theatre in England, in Shoreditch, just beyond London's northern boundary. It was called simply 'The Theatre'. Others soon followed. Thus, when Shakespeare came to London, there were theatres, a flourishing drama and companies of actors waiting for him, such as there had never been before in England. His company performed at James Burbage's Theatre until 1596, and used the Swan and Curtain until they moved into their own new theatre, the Globe, in 1599. It was burnt down in 1613 when a cannon was fired during a performance of Shakespeare's *Henry VIII*.

With the completion in 1996 of Sam Wanamaker's project to construct in London a replica of the Globe, and with productions now running there, a version of Shakespeare's theatre can be experienced at first hand. It is very different to the usual modern experience of drama. The form of the Elizabethan theatre derived from the inn yards and animal baiting rings in which actors had been accustomed to perform in the past. They were circular wooden buildings with a paved courtyard in the middle open to the sky. A rectangular stage jutted out into the middle of this yard. Some of the audience stood in the yard (or 'pit') to watch the play. They were thus on three sides of the stage, close up to it and on a level with it. These 'groundlings' paid only a penny to get in, but for wealthier spectators there were seats in three covered tiers or galleries between the inner and outer walls of the building, extending round most of the auditorium and overlooking the pit and the stage. Such a theatre could hold about three thousand spectators. The yards were about 80ft in diameter and the rectangular stage approximately 40ft by 30ft and 5ft 6 in high. Shakespeare aptly called such a theatre a 'wooden O' in the Prologue to *Henry V* (line 13).

CHECK THE BOOK

The most authoritative book on what we know about the theatre of Shakespeare's time is Andrew Gurr's *The Shakespearean Stage* (CUP, 1992).

CONTEXT

Whereas now, we would conceptualise a visit to the theatre as going to *see* a play, the most common Elizabethan phrase was 'to go *hear* a play' (as in *The Taming of the Shrew*, Induction 2.130) – thus registering the different sensory priorities of the early modern theatre.

THE GLOBE THEATRE,

On the   Bankside.

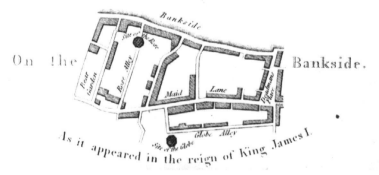

As it appeared in the reign of King James I.

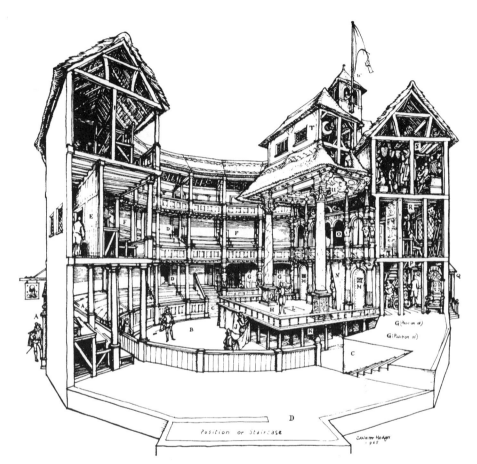

A CONJECTURAL RECONSTRUCTION OF THE INTERIOR OF THE GLOBE PLAYHOUSE

AA Main entrance
B The Yard
CC Entrances to lowest galleries
D Entrance to staircase and upper galleries
E Corridor serving the different sections of the middle gallery
F Middle gallery ('Twopenny Rooms')
G 'Gentlemen's Rooms or Lords Rooms'
H The stage
J The hanging being put up round the stage
K The 'Hell' under the stage
L The stage trap, leading down to the Hell
MM Stage doors

N Curtained 'place behind the stage'
O Gallery above the stage, used as required sometimes by musicians, sometimes by spectators, and often as part of the play
P Back-stage area (the tiring-house)
Q Tiring-house door
R Dressing-rooms
S Wardrobe and storage
T The hut housing the machine for lowering enthroned gods, etc., to the stage
U The 'Heavens'
W Hoisting the playhouse flag

The stage itself was partially covered by a roof or canopy which projected from the wall at the rear of the stage and was supported by two posts at the front. This protected the stage and performers from inclement weather, and to it were secured winches and other machinery for stage effects. On either side at the back of the stage was a door. These led into the dressing room (or 'tiring-house') and it was by means of these doors that actors entered and left the stage. Between these doors was a small recess or alcove which was curtained off. Such a 'discovery place' served, for example, for Juliet's bedroom when in Act IV Scene 4 of *Romeo and Juliet* the Nurse went to the back of the stage and drew the curtain to find, or 'discover' in Elizabethan English, Juliet apparently dead on her bed. Above the discovery place was a balcony, used for the famous balcony scenes of *Romeo and Juliet* (II.2 and III.5), or for the battlements of Richard's castle when he is confronted by Bolingbroke in *Richard II* (III.3). Actors (all parts in the Elizabethan theatre were taken by boys or men) had access to the area beneath the stage; from here, in the 'cellarage', would have come the voice of the ghost of Hamlet's father (*Hamlet*, II.1.150–82).

On these stages there was very little in the way of scenery or props – there was nowhere to store them (there were no wings in this theatre) nor any way to set them up (no tabs across the stage), and, anyway, productions had to be transportable for performance at court or at noble houses. The stage was bare, which is why characters often tell us where they are: there was nothing on the stage to indicate location. It is also why location is so rarely topographical, and much more often symbolic. It suggests a dramatic mood or situation, rather than a place: Lear's barren heath reflects his destitute state, as the storm his emotional turmoil.

None of the plays printed in Shakespeare's lifetime marks act or scene divisions. These have been introduced by later editors, but they should not mislead us into supposing that there was any break in Elizabethan performances such as might happen today while the curtains are closed and the set is changed. The staging of Elizabethan plays was continuous, with the many short 'scenes' of which Shakespeare's plays are often constructed following one after another in quick succession. We have to think of a more fluid and much faster production than we are generally used to: in the

CONTEXT

We do not know much about the props list for a theatre company in Shakespeare's time, although the evidence we do have suggests that there were some quite ambitious examples: one list dating from 1598 includes decorated cloths depicting cities or the night sky, items of armour, horses' heads and 'one hell mouth', probably for performances of Christopher Marlowe's famous play *Doctor Faustus*.

prologues to *Romeo and Juliet* (line 12) and *Henry VIII* (line 13) Shakespeare speaks of only two hours as the playing time. It is because plays were staged continuously that exits and entrances are written in as part of the script: characters speak as they enter or leave the stage because otherwise there would be a silence while, in full view, they took up their positions. (This is also why dead bodies are carried off: they cannot get up and walk off.)

In 1608 Shakespeare's company, the King's Men, acquired the Blackfriars Theatre, a smaller, rectangular indoor theatre, holding about seven hundred people, with seats for all the members of the audience, facilities for elaborate stage effects and, because it was enclosed, artificial lighting. It has been suggested that the plays written for this 'private' theatre differed from those written for the Globe, since, as it cost more to go to a private theatre, the audience came from a higher social stratum and demanded the more elaborate and courtly entertainment which Shakespeare's romances provide. However, the King's Men continued to play in the Globe in the summer, using Blackfriars in the winter, and it is not certain that Shakespeare's last plays were written specifically for the Blackfriars Theatre, or first performed there.

READING SHAKESPEARE

Shakespeare's plays were written for this stage, but there is also a sense in which they were written *by* this stage. The material and physical circumstances of their production in such theatres had a profound effect upon the nature of Elizabethan plays. Unless we bear this in mind, we are likely to find them very strange, for we will read with expectations shaped by our own familiarity with modern fiction and modern drama. This is, by and large, realistic; it seeks to persuade us that what we are reading or watching is really happening. This is quite foreign to Shakespeare. If we try to read him like this, we shall find ourselves irritated by the improbabilities of his plot, confused by his chronology, puzzled by locations, frustrated by unanswered questions and dissatisfied by the motivation of the action. The absurd ease with which disguised persons pass through Shakespeare's plays is a case in point: why does no one recognise people they know so well? There is a great deal of psychological accuracy in Shakespeare's plays, but we are far from any attempt at realism.

CHECK THE BOOK

Deborah Cartmell's *Interpreting Shakespeare on Screen* (Palgrave, 2000) is recommended for its clear and interesting sense of the possibilities and the requirements of approaching Shakespeare through the cinema.

CONTEXT

The Romantic critic Samuel Taylor Coleridge argued that literature requires our 'willing suspension of disbelief': but it is not clear that the theatre of the Shakespearean period did require its audience to forget that they were in a theatre. Certainly, remarks calling attention to the theatrical setting are commonplace – in comedies such as *Twelfth Night* (III.4.125) and *As You Like It* (II.7.139–43), and in tragedies including *Macbeth* (V.5.23–5) – making it more difficult to forget the theatricality of the stories depicted.

The reason is that in Shakespeare's theatre it was impossible to pretend that the audience was not watching a contrived performance. In a modern theatre, the audience is encouraged to forget itself as it becomes absorbed by the action on the stage. The worlds of the spectators and of the actors are sharply distinguished by the lighting: in the dark auditorium the audience is passive, silent, anonymous, receptive and attentive; on the lighted stage the actors are active, vocal, demonstrative and dramatic. (The distinction is, of course, still more marked in the cinema.) There is no communication between the two worlds: for the audience to speak would be interruptive; for the actors to address the audience would be to break the illusion of the play. In the Elizabethan theatre, this distinction did not exist, and for two reasons: first, performances took place in the open air and in daylight which illuminated everyone equally; secondly, the spectators were all around the stage (and wealthier spectators actually on it), and were dressed no differently to the actors, who wore contemporary dress. In such a theatre, spectators would be as aware of each other as of the actors; they could not lose their identity in a corporate group, nor could they ever forget that they were spectators at a performance. There was no chance that they could believe 'this is really happening'.

This, then, was communal theatre, not only in the sense that it was going on in the middle of a crowd but in the sense that the crowd joined in. Elizabethan audiences had none of our deference: they did not keep quiet, or arrive on time, or remain for the whole performance. They joined in, interrupted, even getting on the stage. And plays were preceded and followed by jigs and clowning. It was all much more like our experience of a pantomime, and at a pantomime we are fully aware, and are meant to be aware, that we are watching games being played with reality. The conventions of pantomime revel in their own artificiality: the fishnet tights are to signal that the handsome prince is a woman, the Dame's monstrous false breasts signal that 'she' is a man.

Something very similar is the case with Elizabethan theatre: it utilised its very theatricality. Instead of trying to persuade spectators that they are not in a theatre watching a performance, Elizabethan plays acknowledge the presence of the audience. It is addressed not only by prologues, epilogues and choruses, but in soliloquies. There is no realistic reason why characters should suddenly explain themselves to empty rooms, but, of course, it is not an empty room. The actor is surrounded by people. Soliloquies are not addressed to the world of the play: they are for the audience's benefit. And that audience's complicity is assumed: when a character like Prospero declares himself to be invisible, it is accepted that he is. Disguises are taken to be impenetrable, however improbable, and we are to accept impossibly contrived situations, such as barely hidden characters remaining undetected (indeed, on the Elizabethan stage there was nowhere at all they could hide).

These, then, are plays which are aware of themselves as dramas; in critical terminology, they are self-reflexive, commenting upon themselves as dramatic pieces and prompting the audience to think about the theatrical experience. They do this not only through their direct address to the audience but also through their fondness for the play-within-a-play (which reminds the audience that the encompassing play is also a play) and their constant use of images from, and allusions to, the theatre. They are fascinated by role playing, by acting, appearance and reality. Things are rarely what they seem, either in comedy (for example, in *A Midsummer Night's Dream*) or **tragedy** (*Romeo and Juliet*). This offers one way to think about those disguises: they are thematic rather than realistic. Kent's disguise in *King Lear* reveals his true, loyal self, while Edmund, who is not disguised, hides his true self. In A*s You Like It*, Rosalind is more truly herself disguised as a man than when dressed as a woman.

CHECK THE NET
The 'Designing Shakespeare' database at PADS **(http://www.pads. ahds.ac.uk)** has an extensive collection of photographs from different productions available online.

The effect of all this is to confuse the distinction we would make between 'real life' and 'acting'. The case of Rosalind, for example, raises searching questions about gender roles, about how far it is 'natural' to be womanly or manly: how does the stage, on which a man can play a woman playing a man (and have a man fall in love with him/her), differ from life, in which we assume the roles we think appropriate to masculine and feminine behaviour? The same is true of political roles: when a Richard II or Lear is so aware of the regal part he is performing, of the trappings and rituals of kingship, their plays raise the uncomfortable possibility that the answer to the question of what constitutes a successful king is simply: a good actor. Indeed, human life generally is repeatedly rendered through

READING SHAKESPEARE continued

The poet Walter
Raleigh wrote a
poem on this
image of life as
theatre, which
begins 'What is our
life? A play of
passion', in which
'Our mothers'
wombs the tiring-
houses be, / Where
we are dressed for
this short comedy.'
There's a twist at
the end of the
short verse: 'Only
we die in earnest,
that's no jest.'

the imagery of the stage, from Macbeth's 'Life's but a walking shadow, a poor player / That struts and frets his hour upon the stage / And then is heard no more' (V.5.23-5) to Prospero's paralleling of human life to a performance which, like the globe (both world and theatre), will end (IV.1.146-58). When life is a fiction, like this play, or this play is a fiction like life, what is the difference? 'All the world's a stage ...' (*As You Like It*, II.7.139).

100BC	Caius Julius Caesar is born
75BC	Pirates capture Caesar on his way to Rhodes. After paying the ransom, he hunts the kidnappers down and has them crucified
60BC	The First Triumvirate (an unconstitutional arrangement) is secretly formed to rule the Roman Empire. Caesar joins forces with Crassus, a wealthy banker; and Gnaeus Pompeius (Pompey), a skilful general
59BC	Caesar is elected consul. This furthers his political ambitions and gives him protection from various criminal charges
58–51BC	Gaul is subjugated by Caesar in a campaign that borders on genocide. When Caesar arrives 3 million people live in Gaul. Within six years a million are dead and a further million enslaved. In 55 and 54BC he invades Britain
53BC	Crassus, now governor of Syria, is captured by the Parthians, who kill him by pouring molten gold into his mouth
52BC	Pompey is elected 'consul without colleagues'. The senate demands that Caesar disband his armies
49–46BC	Caesar crosses the river Rubicon and invades Italy. Three years of civil war ensue
48BC	After losing the Battle of Pharsalus, Pompey flees to Egypt, where he is murdered. Caesar becomes Cleopatra's lover
46BC	Victory at Thapsus leaves Caesar undisputed dictator of Rome
44BC	Caesar is murdered in an ostensibly Republican conspiracy headed by Brutus and Cassius. Mark Antony turns public opinion against the conspirators, who are forced to flee Rome. Octavius Caesar, Julius Caesar's 19-year-old adopted son, is denied his inheritance by Antony. While Antony is away fighting Brutus, Octavius Caesar becomes consul. He defeats Antony, but then makes a truce
43BC	Caesar and Antony form the Second Triumvirate with Lepidus
42BC	Antony defeats Cassius and then Brutus at Philippi
40BC	The triumvirs divide the Mediterranean up between them. Antony gets the east (where he forms a liaison with Cleopatra), Octavius the west and Lepidus Africa
36BC	Antony directs disastrous expeditions against the Parthians
32–30BC	The Ptolemaic War. A clever propagandist, Octavius Caesar turns popular opinion against Antony and his Egyptian paramour, and defeats Antony at the Battle of Actium in 31BC
30BC	Alexandria falls to the Romans and Egypt becomes a Roman province
27BC	Octavius Caesar becomes Emperor Augustus. His shrewd reforms lead to 250 years of stability in the Roman Empire

World events	Shakespeare's life	Other literary works
		1516 Thomas More, *Utopia*
1517 Egypt falls to the Ottoman Turks		
		1532 Niccolò Machiavelli, *The Prince* (published posthumously)
1543 Copernicus challenges accepted views on astronomy (formulated in Ptolemaic Egypt) and his work is banned by the Catholic Church		
	1557 John Shakespeare marries Mary Arden	
1558 The French capture Calais, ending 210 years of English possession		
	1564 Born in Stratford-upon-Avon	
1565 Sir John Hawkins brings tobacco to England		
1576 First theatre in England opens at Shoreditch		
		1578 Robert Garnier, *Marc Antoine* (in French)
		1579 Thomas North translates Plutarch's *Lives of the Noble Grecians and Romans*
1581 Conversion to Roman Catholicism is deemed treason in England		
1582 Plague breaks out in London	**1582** Marries Anne Hathaway	
1583 Newfoundland is claimed for Elizabeth I by Humphrey Gilbert	**1583** A daughter, Susanna, is born	
	1585 The twins, Hamnet and Judith, are born	

World events	Shakespeare's life	Other literary works
1588 Spanish Armada defeated	**late 1580s – early 1590s** Shakespeare probably writes *Henry VI*, parts 1, 2 and 3, and *Richard III*	
		1590 Christopher Marlowe, *Dido, Queen of Carthage*
	1592 Shakespeare acting in London	**1592** Garnier's *Marc Antoine* translated into English
	1592–4 Writes *The Comedy of Errors*	
1593–1606 Ottoman expansion into Europe halted by prolonged war with Austria	**1594** Writes exclusively for the Lord Chamberlain's Men	**1594** Samuel Daniel, *The Tragedie of Cleopatra*
1595–1603 Tyrone's rebellion in Ireland	**1595** *Two Gentlemen of Verona, The Taming of the Shrew* and *Love's Labour's Lost* are thought to have been completed by this time. Writes *Romeo and Juliet*	
1596 Francis Drake perishes on an expedition to the West Indies	**1596–8** *Henry IV*, parts 1 and 2, written	
1598 First mention of the game of cricket	**1598–9** Globe Theatre built at Southwark	
	1599 *Henry V* completed	
	1600 *A Midsummer Night's Dream, Much Ado about Nothing* and *The Merchant of Venice* printed. *Twelfth Night* and *Julius Caesar* probably written	
	1600–1 *Hamlet* written	

World events

1603 Elizabeth I dies

1605 Discovery of Guy Fawkes's plot to destroy Parliament

1607 English Parliament rejects union between England and Scotland

1609 Tea is introduced into Europe by the Dutch

1610 Use of the fork for eating spreads from Italy to England

1612 Last burning of heretics in England

1620 The *Mayflower* takes the Pilgrim Fathers to Massachusetts

Shakespeare's life

1602 *Troilus and Cressida* probably written

1603 His company becomes the King's Men, patronised by James I, the new king

1604 *Othello* performed

1605 First version of *King Lear*

1606 Writes *Macbeth*

1606–7 *Antony and Cleopatra* probably written

1608 The King's Men acquire Blackfriars Theatre for winter performances

1610 *Coriolanus* written

1611 Shakespeare retires to his house in Stratford

1613 Globe Theatre burns down

1616 Shakespeare dies

Other literary works

1604 James I, *A Counterblast to Tobacco*

1605 Cervantes, *Don Quixote*

1606 Ben Jonson, *Volpone*

1612 John Webster, *The White Devil*

1677 John Dryden, *All for Love, or the World Well Lost*

SHAKESPEARE'S SOURCES FOR *ANTONY AND CLEOPATRA*

Geoffrey Bullough (ed.), *Narrative and Dramatic Sources of Shakespeare*, vol. 5, 'The Roman Plays', Macmillan, 1964
> This is the standard work, containing the main sources, chiefly Plutarch's 'Life of Antony' but also passages from other Roman lives by Plutarch, represented in North's translation of 1579

T. J. B. Spencer (ed.), *Shakespeare's Plutarch*, Penguin Books, 1964
> This handy volume contains the relevant lives in North's Plutarch with passages from Shakespeare keyed into the text. It also has a brief glossary

CRITICISM

Janet Adelman, *The Common Liar: An Essay on Antony and Cleopatra*, Yale University Press, 1973
> A lucid account that, like that of Mason below, sees a disjunction between the action and the poetry but argues that this is deliberate and stresses the double and sometimes problematic view the play offers of its protagonists in love and politics

Janet Adelman, *Suffocating Mothers: Fantasies of Maternal Origin in Shakespeare's Plays*, Routledge, 1992

A. C. Bradley, *Shakespearean Tragedy*, Macmillan, 1904

Reuben A. Brower, *Hero and Saint: Shakespeare and the Graeco-Roman Heroic Tradition*, Oxford University Press, 1971
> Traditional criticism that discusses the plays in the light of the Renaissance reception of the epics of Homer and Virgil and other Roman sources

John Russell Brown (ed.), *Shakespeare: Antony and Cleopatra* (Casebook Series), Macmillan, 1968; revised edition, 1991
> As well as containing a selection of earlier criticism and a number of reviews of the play in performance from 1849 to 1987, this volume contains an anthology of influential twentieth-century criticism, starting with A. C. Bradley's much referred to lecture of 1909 (see **Critical history**)

Jonathan Dollimore, *Radical Tragedy: Religion, Ideology and Power in the Drama of Shakespeare and His Contemporaries*, Harvester Press, 1984

FURTHER READING

John Drakakis (ed.), *Antony and Cleopatra* (New Casebooks), Macmillan, 1994
   A substantial introduction brings to bear the perspectives of recent theoretical approaches to the play

Marilyn French, *Shakespeare's Division of Experience*, Jonathan Cape, 1982

Harley Granville-Barker, *Prefaces to Shakespeare*, vol. 3, Sidgewick & Jackson, 1930; reprinted by Batsford, 1963 and 1972
   A theatrical producer responsible for one of the first modern productions of the text as we have it, the author provides a defence of the play's structure as something that can work well on stage

Graham Holderness, Bryan Loughrey and Andrew Murphy (eds.), *Shakespeare: The Roman Plays*, Longman, 1996
   In the Longman Critical Reader Series, there are three essays on the play falling within the New Historicist/Cultural Materialist critical spectrum

Coppélia Kahn, *Roman Shakespeare: Warriors, Wounds, and Women*, Routledge, 1997
   In a series called Feminist Readings of Shakespeare, this sets all the Roman works in the dual context of the popular theatre and Renaissance humanism from a feminist perspective

G. Wilson Knight, *The Imperial Theme*, Oxford University Press, 1931; revised edition Methuen, 1954
   Analyses the themes and poetic structure, and presents a very positive view of the transcendent power of the love affair in the play

H. A. Mason, *Shakespeare's Tragedies of Love*, Chatto and Windus, 1970
   Two substantial chapters, one of which has the title 'Telling versus Shewing', take a sceptical view of the dramatic effectiveness of the poetry and argue that the play is not taken to a fully tragic conclusion

Robert S. Miola, *Shakespeare's Rome*, Cambridge University Press, 1983

Brian Vickers (ed.), *William Shakespeare: The Critical Heritage*, 6 vols., Routledge, 1974
   This is the fullest compilation of Shakespeare criticism arranged chronologically from the seventeenth century through to the nineteenth. The judgements of earlier writers (for example, those of Johnson, Coleridge and Hazlitt mentioned in **Critical history**) can be found here. Through use of the indices readers can construct their own account of the evolving critical response to the play. It includes notices of early performances

Nigel Wood (ed.), *Antony and Cleopatra* (Theory in Practice), Open University Press, 1996
   A volume in the Theory in Practice series that has four essays discussing the play in the light of a theory of doubles, post-colonialism, feminism and genre criticism

GENERAL READING

Benedict Anderson, *Imagined Communities*, Verso Books, revised edition, 1991

T. W. Baldwin, *William Shakspere's Smalle Latine and Lesse Greeke*, University of Illinois Press, 1944

Deborah Cartmell, *Interpreting Shakespeare on Screen*, Palgrave, 2000

Wolfgang Clemen, *The Development of Shakespeare's Imagery*, Methuen, 1951

John Drakakis and Naomi Conn Liebler (eds.), *Tragedy*, Longman, 1998

Andrew Gurr, *The Shakespearean Stage*, Cambridge University Press, 1992

Sister Miriam Joseph, *Rhetoric in Shakespeare's Time*, Harcourt, 1962

Frank Kermode, *Shakespeare's Language*, Penguin, 2000

Richard Lanham, *A Handbook of Rhetorical Terms: A Guide for Students of English Literature*, University of California Press, 1969

M. M. Mahood, *Shakespeare's Wordplay*, Methuen, 1957

C. T. Onions, *A Shakespeare Glossary*, Oxford University Press, 1911 (frequently reprinted)

Eric Partridge, *Shakespeare's Bawdy: A Literary and Psychological Essay*, Routledge & Kegan Paul, 1955

Edward W. Said, *Orientalism: Western Concepts of the Orient*, Routledge & Kegan Paul, 1978

Samuel Schoenbaum, *Shakespeare: A Documentary Life*, Oxford University Press, 1975

Caroline F. E. Spurgeon, *Shakespeare's Imagery and What It Tells Us*, Cambridge University Press, 1935

Stanley Wells and Lena Cowen Orlin (eds.), *Shakespeare: An Oxford Guide*, Oxford University Press, 2003

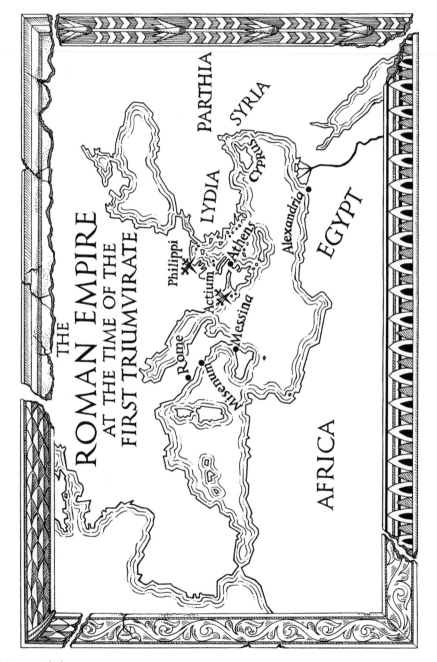

THE
ROMAN EMPIRE
AT THE TIME OF THE
FIRST TRIUMVIRATE

PARTHIA

SYRIA

LYDIA

Cyprus

Philippi

Athens

Actium

Alexandria

EGYPT

Messina

Rome

Misenum

AFRICA

anachronism from the Greek meaning 'referring to the wrong time', as when Cleopatra proposes playing billiards (II.5.3), a game of Shakespeare's time that had not been invented in the period in which the play is set

antithesis from the Greek meaning 'opposite placing'. A rhetorical term describing the opposition of contrasting ideas in neighbouring sentences or clauses, using opposite or contrasting forms of words: 'In me 'tis villainy; / In thee't had been good service' (II.7.74–5). The word can be used more loosely to describe a structural or thematic contrast, as when the world of Rome is deliberately contrasted with the world of Egypt in the play

conceit from the Latin meaning 'thought', an image that appeals to the intellect. A witty, ingenious and far-fetched comparison, often extended in its application: 'Why, sir, give the gods a thankful sacrifice. When it pleaseth their deities to take the wife of a man from him, it shows to man the tailors of the earth; comforting therein that when old robes are worn out there are members to make new. If there were no more women but Fulvia, then had you indeed a cut, and the case to be lamented. This grief is crowned with consolation: your old smock brings forth a new petticoat; and indeed the tears live in an onion that should water this sorrow' (I.2.162–71)

figure of speech from the Latin meaning 'to shape, form or conceive'. Any form of expression or grammar which deviates from the plainest expression of meaning; such figures may be metaphor, simile, antithesis, hyperbole, oxymoron, paradox and many others

hyperbole from the Greek meaning 'excess, exaggeration'. Exaggerated or extravagant language used for emphasis and not intended to be understood literally; self-conscious exaggeration: 'His legs bestrid the ocean' (V.2.82)

neoclassical from the Greek word for new and the Latin word 'classic'; an adjective used to denote in the Renaissance and seventeenth and eighteenth centuries any literature and art that sought to conform to the rules or models of Greek or Latin antiquity. The literature of the period from 1660 to 1750 is particularly marked by this tendency. Dryden's *All for Love, or The World Well Lost* (1677) is constructed on neoclassical principles, that is, it obeys the rules supposedly derived from and embodied in the masterpieces of ancient tragedy; it maintains the unities and it does not mix the genres of comedy and tragedy. Judged by neoclassical standards, *Antony and Cleopatra* is an irregular play

oxymoron from the Greek meaning 'pointedly foolish'. A witty paradoxical expression often containing a conjunction of opposites, like 'bittersweet': 'Royal wench!' (II.2.231)

LITERARY TERMS

paradox from the Greek meaning 'contrary to opinion or expectation'. A seemingly self-contradictory statement, which yet is shown to be (sometimes in a surprising way) true: 'for with a wound I must be cured' (IV.14.78)

simile from the Latin meaning 'like'. An explicit comparison, for instance: 'Those his goody eyes, / That o'er the files and musters of the war / Have glowed like plated Mars' (I.1.2–4)

tragedy from the Greek meaning 'goat song' (an unhelpful derivation). The traditional account in Aristotle's *Poetics*, written about 340BC and rediscovered in the Renaissance, stressed that it featured persons of high status undergoing a change of fortune; in the best sort of tragedy the protagonist, a person neither wholly good nor wholly bad but of moderate character like Oedipus in Sophocles' *King Oedipus* (431BC), falls from greatness through some error. Aristotle's word for error, *hamartia*, is sometimes translated as 'tragic flaw', but it may not be a moral flaw, simply a mistake. This error leads to catastrophe and ultimately to a recognition or self-discovery, and the suffering involved causes the spectators to experience pity and fear from their involvement with the tragic character resulting in a catharsis, a purgation or purification of the emotions. Many traditional discussions of the play tacitly assume such a notion of the tragic experience and effect in their account

tragicomedy a play, like *Antony and Cleopatra*, that mingles elements of both **tragedy** and comedy (for instance, characters of high and low status) which were always kept distinct in antiquity

unities in his account of Greek tragedy in the *Poetics*, Aristotle observes that plays concentrate upon one complete action and that the plots representing this single action are bound together by a chain of cause and effect in a probable or necessary sequence, that they take place in one setting and that they tend to cover a time period of little more than one revolution of the sun. From these observations are derived the dramatic unities of action, time and place. Under classical influence they acquired a special authority in the Renaissance. The only play of Shakespeare that obeys the unities is his last play, *The Tempest*

AUTHOR OF THESE NOTES

Robin Sowerby studied Classics and English at Cambridge. He now lectures in the Department of English Studies at Stirling University. He has written York Notes on Homer's *Iliad* and *Odyssey*, Virgil's *Aeneid* and Plato's *Republic*. He has edited selections from Dryden and Pope and is the author of *The Classical Legacy in Renaissance Poetry*, Longman, 1994.

General editor

Martin Gray, former Head of the Department of English Studies at the University of Stirling, and of Literary Studies at the University of Luton.

Maya Angelou
I Know Why the Caged Bird Sings

Jane Austen
Pride and Prejudice

Alan Ayckbourn
Absent Friends

Elizabeth Barrett Browning
Selected Poems

Robert Bolt
A Man for All Seasons

Harold Brighouse
Hobson's Choice

Charlotte Brontë
Jane Eyre

Emily Brontë
Wuthering Heights

Shelagh Delaney
A Taste of Honey

Charles Dickens
David Copperfield
Great Expectations
Hard Times
Oliver Twist

Roddy Doyle
Paddy Clarke Ha Ha Ha

George Eliot
Silas Marner
The Mill on the Floss

Anne Frank
The Diary of a Young Girl

William Golding
Lord of the Flies

Oliver Goldsmith
She Stoops to Conquer

Willis Hall
The Long and the Short and the Tall

Thomas Hardy
Far from the Madding Crowd
The Mayor of Casterbridge
Tess of the d'Urbervilles
The Withered Arm and other Wessex Tales

L.P. Hartley
The Go-Between

Seamus Heaney
Selected Poems

Susan Hill
I'm the King of the Castle

Barry Hines
A Kestrel for a Knave

Louise Lawrence
Children of the Dust

Harper Lee
To Kill a Mockingbird

Laurie Lee
Cider with Rosie

Arthur Miller
The Crucible
A View from the Bridge

Robert O'Brien
Z for Zachariah

Frank O'Connor
My Oedipus Complex and Other Stories

George Orwell
Animal Farm

J.B. Priestley
An Inspector Calls
When We Are Married

Willy Russell
Educating Rita
Our Day Out

J.D. Salinger
The Catcher in the Rye

William Shakespeare
Henry IV Part I
Henry V
Julius Caesar
Macbeth
The Merchant of Venice
A Midsummer Night's Dream
Much Ado About Nothing
Romeo and Juliet
The Tempest
Twelfth Night

George Bernard Shaw
Pygmalion

Mary Shelley
Frankenstein

R.C. Sherriff
Journey's End

Rukshana Smith
Salt on the snow

John Steinbeck
Of Mice and Men

Robert Louis Stevenson
Dr Jekyll and Mr Hyde

Jonathan Swift
Gulliver's Travels

Robert Swindells
Daz 4 Zoe

Mildred D. Taylor
Roll of Thunder, Hear My Cry

Mark Twain
Huckleberry Finn

James Watson
Talking in Whispers

Edith Wharton
Ethan Frome

William Wordsworth
Selected Poems

A Choice of Poets

Mystery Stories of the Nineteenth Century including The Signalman

Nineteenth Century Short Stories

Poetry of the First World War

Six Women Poets

For the AQA Anthology:
Duffy and Armitage & Pre-1914 Poetry

Heaney and Clarke & Pre-1914 Poetry

Poems from Different Cultures

Margaret Atwood
Cat's Eye
The Handmaid's Tale

Jane Austen
Emma
Mansfield Park
Persuasion
Pride and Prejudice
Sense and Sensibility

Alan Bennett
Talking Heads

William Blake
Songs of Innocence and of Experience

Charlotte Brontë
Jane Eyre
Villette

Emily Brontë
Wuthering Heights

Angela Carter
Nights at the Circus

Geoffrey Chaucer
The Franklin's Prologue and Tale
The Merchant's Prologue and Tale
The Miller's Prologue and Tale
The Prologue to the Canterbury Tales
The Wife of Bath's Prologue and Tale

Samuel Coleridge
Selected Poems

Joseph Conrad
Heart of Darkness

Daniel Defoe
Moll Flanders

Charles Dickens
Bleak House
Great Expectations
Hard Times

Emily Dickinson
Selected Poems

John Donne
Selected Poems

Carol Ann Duffy
Selected Poems

George Eliot
Middlemarch
The Mill on the Floss

T.S. Eliot
Selected Poems
The Waste Land

F. Scott Fitzgerald
The Great Gatsby

E.M. Forster
A Passage to India

Brian Friel
Translations

Thomas Hardy
Jude the Obscure
The Mayor of Casterbridge
The Return of the Native
Selected Poems
Tess of the d'Urbervilles

Seamus Heaney
Selected Poems from 'Opened Ground'

Nathaniel Hawthorne
The Scarlet Letter

Homer
The Iliad
The Odyssey

Aldous Huxley
Brave New World

Kazuo Ishiguro
The Remains of the Day

Ben Jonson
The Alchemist

James Joyce
Dubliners

John Keats
Selected Poems

Philip Larkin
The Whitsun Weddings and Selected Poems

Christopher Marlowe
Doctor Faustus
Edward II

Arthur Miller
Death of a Salesman

John Milton
Paradise Lost Books I & II

Toni Morrison
Beloved

George Orwell
Nineteen Eighty-Four

Sylvia Plath
Selected Poems

Alexander Pope
Rape of the Lock & Selected Poems

William Shakespeare
Antony and Cleopatra
As You Like It
Hamlet
Henry IV Part I
King Lear
Macbeth
Measure for Measure
The Merchant of Venice
A Midsummer Night's Dream
Much Ado About Nothing
Othello
Richard II
Richard III
Romeo and Juliet
The Taming of the Shrew
The Tempest
Twelfth Night
The Winter's Tale

George Bernard Shaw
Saint Joan

Mary Shelley
Frankenstein

Jonathan Swift
Gulliver's Travels and A Modest Proposal

Alfred Tennyson
Selected Poems

Virgil
The Aeneid

Alice Walker
The Color Purple

Oscar Wilde
The Importance of Being Earnest

Tennessee Williams
A Streetcar Named Desire
The Glass Menagerie

Jeanette Winterson
Oranges Are Not the Only Fruit

John Webster
The Duchess of Malfi

Virginia Woolf
To the Lighthouse

William Wordsworth
The Prelude and Selected Poems

W.B. Yeats
Selected Poems

Metaphysical Poets